THE NEW TEACHER

An Introduction to Teaching in Comprehensive Education

NIGEL TUBBS

David Fulton Publishers
London

David Fulton Publishers Ltd
2 Barbon Close, London WC1N 3JX

First published in Great Britain by
David Fulton Publishers 1996

Note: The right of Nigel Tubbs to be identified as the author of this work has
been asserted by him in accordance with the Copyright, Designs and Patents
Act 1988.

Copyright © Nigel Tubbs

British Library Cataloguing in Publication Data

A catalogue record for this book is available from the British Library

ISBN 1-85346–424–4

Typeset by The Harrington Consultancy
Printed in Great Britain by BPC Books and Journals Ltd, Exeter

Contents

Series Editor's Foreword

This book takes as its starting-point the fact that in most parts of Britain, the majority of 11-16-year-olds receive their education in comprehensive schools which therefore also both train and provide employment for the vast majority of people entering the teaching profession.

Yet, despite this self-evident truth, there is a paucity of material articulating the philosophy and practice of comprehensive schooling for new teachers. And it is therefore most welcome that this book should attempt to relate classroom practice to the aims of comprehensive education as a whole. It is indeed one of the peculiarities of the situation in this country that so little regard should be paid to the concept of pedagogy, with our whole approach to educational theory and practice being both amateurish and highly pragmatic in character.

In this short but wide-ranging book, Nigel Tubbs provides ample material for debate about the "how" and the "why" of classroom practice. Throughout, the emphasis is on relating that practice to a definition of comprehensive education that embraces everyone and which guarantees the entitlement to education of all children in our society.

Clyde Chitty
Birmingham
January 1996

Dedication

I dedicate this book to my mother, Mrs Barbara Brown.

Preface

A fully comprehensive education system has yet to be achieved. Equally, the aims, the principles and the pedagogies of comprehensive education have not been fully explored, either in theory or in practice. Nevertheless, and perhaps because of this, a book outlining the philosophy and practice of comprehensive education for new teachers is long overdue.

It is the case that most new teachers train and work in comprehensive schools, and that most parents have their children educated in comprehensive schools. Yet despite this, there are very few books currently available to new teachers which relate classroom competences and teacher training to the aims and objectives of the comprehensive system as a whole. In addition, there are frequent attempts to undermine comprehensive education, for example, by reintroducing selection and/or market forces into the education system. In the face of such attacks, it is necessary and timely to restate the case that only a comprehensive system, and its (new) teachers, can address the needs of *all* children, and fulfil their unconditional entitlement to free primary and secondary education. *The New Teacher* is written for those who already work to realize that entitlement, and for those who wish to begin to do so.

With thanks to Sue, Pete and Pete at Thomas Bennett Community College, Crawley; Mick and Anne at Countesthorpe College, Leicestershire; Adrian and Liz at Patcham High School, Brighton; Mike at Oaklands in Southampton; Fiona at Hampden Park School, Eastbourne; Jess and Sheila at Icon Bennett; Anne Judd at King Alfred's College, Winchester; and in memory of Gillian Rose, professor of social and political thought at Warwick University, who died on 9 December 1995 after a long struggle with cancer. She was, and still is, my teacher.

Nigel Tubbs
Winchester
January 1996

QUALITY IN SECONDARY SCHOOLS AND COLLEGES SERIES

Series Editor: Clyde Chitty

This series publishes on a wide range of topics related to successful education for the 11–19 age group. It reflects the growing interest in whole-school curriculum planning together with the effective teaching of individual subjects and themes. There are also books devoted to management and administration, examinations and assessment, pastoral care strategies, relationships with parents and governors and the implications for schools of changes in teacher education. Titles include:

'The truth of the independent consciousness is... the servile
consciousness of the bondsman.'

(Hegel, 1977, p 117)

Introduction

Comprehensive education and comprehensive schools are, in the main, only 30 years old. Universal entitlement to free education for all children is itself only 50 years old. Before that, high quality education was available to a small minority of children whose parents could afford to pay the fees. In 1944, the state took responsibility for making education available to all, regardless of the ability of parents to pay. But it set up different sorts of schools for pupils who, according to their performance in the 11 plus, were deemed to have different mental aptitudes and abilities. Selection according to wealth was replaced by selection according to IQ levels. In response to the inequalities of the selective system, several local education authorities began to reorganize along comprehensive lines in the 1950s. Circular 10/65, issued during the Wilson government, demanded that *all* authorities submit plans for such a reorganization.

The selective system (notably private schools, grammar schools and most likely 'opted out' schools) and the comprehensive system have fundamentally different outlooks. A selective system only has to meet the specific demands of a certain clientele. A school decides the criteria upon which its pupils will be selected, and rejects the others. Its *product* is designed for a niche market.

This outlook is contrary to the comprehensive system which seeks to offer education to *all* children, having no predetermined criteria for their eligibility. Comprehensive means a system that embraces everyone, that is universal and unconditional, and which guarantees the entitlement to education of all children. State schools are charged with putting this promise of universal entitlement into practice, and with making it a reality. Just as the state cannot choose who it will and will not educate, neither can its comprehensive schools. The comprehensive teacher is the front-line worker in establishing and realizing this service.

When new teachers join comprehensive schools, either for their teaching practice or as newly qualified teachers (NQTs), they become part of that commitment to universal entitlement. They have to work within the responsibilities and obligations which that commitment imposes. Whilst teachers in selective schools are asked to offer a specifically designed product to a preselected group of clients, teachers in comprehensive schools are asked to offer a full service to all who are entitled to it, and one which can be designed and redesigned to meet the needs of all who require it.

Because the state does not recognize the entitlement of any one child to be greater or less than that of any other, so comprehensive teachers are obliged to acknowledge the education of each child as of *equal value*. For new teachers, this equates with the ability to plan and to teach lessons which give the best possible chance of success to pupils at all ages and at all levels of ability. This involves competence in forming relationships, in selecting appropriate teaching styles, in differentiation, and in classroom management. In addition, valuing pupils equally means valuing pupils for who they are, not only in respect of their abilities and talents, but also for their weaknesses and limitations. In what follows, then, equal value in a comprehensive system of educational entitlement forms the professional standard against which classroom practice and responsibilities for the new teacher are explored.

Too often, books for new teachers give tips on the 'how' of classroom practice without relating that practice to the aims of the service as a whole. One of the intentions of *The New Teacher* is the drawing together of discussions about how to teach with the responsibilities and obligations which such decisions must fulfil. New teachers receive an incomplete and therefore unprofessional perspective when considerations of teaching method are kept separate from the commitment to universal entitlement and equal value. *The New Teacher* combines in one voice the skills and competences expected of new teachers, and the professional considerations which they must take account of in performing those skills and competences. The actual practice of teachers and the professional responsibilities of teachers are presented here as one indivisible set of considerations.

Structure

The New Teacher is for those new to teaching in comprehensive schools, be they on initial teacher training or NQTs, and for their school-based mentors. The text provides material for discussion and debate about the how and the why of classroom practice. Each chapter has a selection of readings which complement the text, designed to aid professional discussion. The book should also provide material for seminar-based work in colleges and universities for those on B.Ed and PGCE courses.

The New Teacher is best read from the beginning. It is not designed for dipping into. The arrangement of the chapters tries to anticipate problems and issues in the order in which they often occur although, of course, there can be no predetermination of such things. Chapter 1 looks at the sort of planning and preparation which is appropriate before joining a school. Chapter 2 explores the working relationships which will be expected. Chapters 3 and 4 examine classroom practice and some of the issues raised when teaching has begun. Chapter 5 looks at the often ignored role of the tutor. Chapter 6, about 'control' in the classroom, is deliberately left until the end. There are no short-cuts to learning how to manage a group. Control is itself based upon sound planning and preparation, good relationships, appropriate pedagogy, careful differentiation, and valuing pupils. The reason for leaving the chapter until the end, therefore, is to give the strong message that control is the *result* of good practice, not independent of it.

Introductions to teaching for new teachers often make much of the idea of 'survival'. Such an approach sells teachers and their profession short. Teachers who are clear about the aims and philosophy of comprehensive education understand that their practice involves a great deal more than 'personal survival'. Above all else, it involves planning for the success of their pupils, which itself will ensure success for the teacher. What follows, then, does *not* offer a guide to survival for the new teacher. It takes what it holds to be the more professional approach of exploring how the responsibility for ensuring pupil entitlement can be translated into effective and successful practice for the new teacher.

CHAPTER ONE

Preparation and Planning

Self-preparation

Preparation for becoming a teacher, whether as a student on teaching practice, or as a newly qualified teacher (NQT), takes a number of different forms. At a philosophical level, new teachers require some self-preparation regarding the nature of comprehensive education. One important aspect of this is trying to avoid prejudging what one hopes or expects it to be like. At the most general level, new teachers need to accept and understand that they will be required to teach a comprehensive range of pupils, differing in terms of ability, attitude, personality, background, language, motivation, parental support, sense of humour and behaviour. Preparation for this involves new teachers overcoming preconceptions about what constitutes a 'good' pupil in order to avoid being resentful should their real pupils not match up to this. What is important for new teachers is that they have an open mind about their pupils, and allow themselves to be surprised and excited by the variety of pupils which comprehensive schools offer.

An equally important form of self-preparation for new teachers is sociological. This requires them quickly to become acquainted with what it is like to work within schools as *institutions*. As with any institution, schools have ways of doing things, established rituals and practices, and expectations of their personnel in terms of dress, behaviour and levels of formality and informality. In all schools, a particular expectation of teachers is that they accept the need to 'fit in' with these established rhythms and patterns of working. Few schools expect their teachers to 'sell their souls' in conforming to institutional demands, but a *compromise* between individuality and conformity is expected. This is most apparent in terms of dress codes and the levels of formality and informality used when talking to other staff and to pupils.

A third form of self-preparation is reflective. Anyone entering the teaching profession needs to reflect carefully on what teachers are actually expected and obliged to do. Teachers occupy a middle position between what is to be learnt and who is to learn it. The most important form of preparation and planning which teachers can engage in *from their pupils' point of view* is to ensure that courses and lessons are designed with the pupils' needs and abilities in mind. The self-preparation of new teachers therefore includes the recognition that it will be their job to decide *how* the course material and the pupils are to be brought together, and the realization that such pedagogical decisions can determine whether pupils experience success, failure, or just plain boredom.

A corollary of this reflection on what it is to be a teacher is, in the first instance, a reflection on what it is to become a *student* teacher. Student teachers have a dual role, being both teacher and student. They are required not only to teach, but also to learn. Mentors are soon suspicious of, and unsympathetic to, student teachers who think they know everything and refuse to seek or take advice. Student teachers have to fulfil their role as a learner by asking questions, by listening, by seeking support, by accepting criticism, and by acting upon any help and advice that is offered. The person who is both a student and a teacher lives out a very difficult, ambiguous and unsettled existence, never able to achieve a position as one or the other. One reminder of this lack of a secure identity is the often heard question from pupils, 'Are you a real teacher?' As a student teacher there are no easy ways of avoiding this public exposure of being someone who is, in fact, training to become someone else.

Teacher/learner

What am I really doing? And why am I doing it? – that is the question of truth which is not taught in our present system of education and is consequently not asked; we have no time for it.

(Nietzsche, 1982, pp.196–197)

He who learns *bestows talent upon himself* – only it is not so easy to learn; and not only a matter of having the will to do so; one also has to be able to learn.

(Nietzsche, 1982, p.541)

The only man who is educated is the man who has learned how to learn; the man who has learned how to adapt and change; the man who has realised that no knowledge is secure, that only the process of seeking knowledge gives a basis for security.

(Rogers, 1969, p.104)

> Teaching is more difficult than learning because what teaching calls for is this: to let learn. The real teacher, in fact, lets nothing else be learned than learning....
>
> The teacher must be capable of being more teachable than the apprentices....If the relation between the teacher and the learners is genuine, therefore, there is never a place in it for the authority of the know-it-all or the authoritative sway of the official. It is an exalted matter, then, to become a teacher....
>
> (Heidegger, in Krell, 1977, p.356)

Finally, like all students, student teachers and NQTs need to prepare for themselves and their performance in schools to be publicly assessed and evaluated. This can be a very threatening prospect for new teachers, many of whom will be used to success in written examinations, but inexperienced in any forms of personal appraisal.

The forms of self-preparation mentioned so far have been preparations of mind and of attitude. There are also more concrete forms of preparation which new teachers, but, in particular, student teachers on teaching practice have to undertake.

First, student teachers are required to become familiar with the courses which they will be teaching. There are several stages to this. They need to understand the course as a whole, to understand the learning outcomes which it seeks to realize, to know how long the course is intended to last, to know exactly what it is that pupils are being asked to do on the course, and to know the form in which the pupils' work is to be presented and assessed. Then they are required to concentrate on that part of the course (it may well be the whole course) which they will be given responsibility for. This means having in advance all the resources which are used on the course, and, if necessary, adding to them. To teach a course which has been put together by someone else imposes its own set of challenges, and to teach only part of that course, even more so. To do so effectively requires all teachers to ensure that their planning includes their achieving a thorough familiarity with (some would say 'ownership' of) all aspects of the course.

Second, the preparation of student teachers includes becoming familiar with the organization of the school day, ensuring that they know who is supposed to be where, at what time, and for what reason.

Third, having received their timetables, student teachers are advised to try and obtain relevant information about the groups they will be teaching, in particular with regard to the spread of levels of ability, and any pupils with previously identified special needs. It can be very helpful to have sight of previous work which these groups have produced. An equally important form of preparation is to observe as many lessons as possible. Often student teachers are sceptical about the value of this, and impatient to begin their own teaching. But, as Chapter 2 will show, patience in this regard is very important. Observing other teachers is a most valuable form of preparation. Of particular importance are observations regarding how lessons are begun and ended, different styles of teaching, different methods of dealing with problems, and different types of activities given to the pupils. With an increasing sophistication, student teachers may well begin to observe how various teachers achieve *differentiation,* how they seek to make work relevant to all ability levels, and how they ensure that pupil learning is developing and progressing.

Lesson planning

The first thing student teachers can expect to be asked to plan are their lessons. The lesson plan is not the most popular aspect of teaching practice. For one thing, student teachers seem to be expected to produce them in great detail whereas experienced teachers may boast of not having done one for years. University and college tutors place great emphasis upon them, mentors also, and yet having produced one, student teachers may well find themselves criticized either for sticking to it too rigidly or for not following it closely enough. Some who see it may think there is too much written down and expect students to be able to think more on their feet and respond more freely in the classroom; others may demand that they write down in advance a great deal and ad lib as little as possible. And, perhaps most frustrating of all, some mentors may want their students to break the lesson down into five- or ten-minute slots, with each bit planned and accounted for in the lesson plan whilst for others, such strict packaging is anathema to learning, and they will expect students to respond flexibly according to the needs of the lesson at any particular point. Preparation at this level should therefore include discussing lesson plans with mentors to ensure that the methods of planning employed by students are not too far from the expectations of those who will judge their performance.

However, there are certain *professional* considerations with regard to lesson planning which override these individual preferences. A lesson plan needs to include the *why, what, when* and *how* of the lesson. Without due consideration of each of these, student teachers could be seen to be underprepared for their lessons.

Why?

With any lesson plan, student teachers ought to be able to show that they understand *why* they are teaching this lesson, that is, its place in the structure of the course overall. The lesson plan should always state, however briefly, how the *objectives* of this particular lesson contribute to fulfilling the *aims* of the course overall. Most importantly, the lesson plan needs to be specific in terms of the learning outcomes which it intends for the pupils. A mentor will want to be able to see that student teachers have thought about what they want their pupils to learn in a lesson, and therefore to be able to judge whether those intended outcomes have been realized.

What?

It is useful in lesson plans to list all the resources which will be required; that is, *what* the teacher and the pupils are going to need, and to check their availability beforehand. If new resources are required, ideally they should be produced in time to show them to someone else for their comments and, if appropriate, offered to colleagues for them to use as well. This requires planning well in advance, but it is a very visible activity and one which shows student teachers are taking their planning and preparation seriously.

When?

A lesson plan ought to show that teachers have thought about the amount of work which they will try to get through in the lesson, and that they know, at least approximately, *when* each activity will need to begin and how long each should last.

Timing is a common source of frustration for student teachers. Too little content leaves time at the end in which classroom management can suddenly become a problem. Too much content is by far the best option, providing it is remembered that teachers do not need to get through all of the content just because they have prepared it. Some of the content may only be useful for the pupils who work more quickly than expected. The greater their experience, the better able teachers become to judge the amount of work which can sensibly be included in a single lesson. It is always worth asking someone how much they would expect to get through in a lesson rather than just guessing or hoping. It is common, to begin with, for student teachers to be surprised at how little work some pupils are able to get through in a lesson.

How?

The most important part of any lesson plan is the *how*. Teachers may know what they are going to do, and why, and when in the time available they are going to do it, but success and effectiveness depend on *how* it is done. The method chosen for presenting the content of the lesson will be the key factor in determining how successful the lesson is. Teachers are the *mediators* between the curriculum and the pupil. It is their professional responsibility to choose the most effective means available for bringing the pupil and the content together to ensure that the former is successful in learning from the latter (see Chapter 3). A lesson plan should reveal that student teachers have thought about some of the different ways of presenting the content, and can justify the choices they have made.

Some lesson plans might, for example, say only,

10.00 – 10.15 Explain how a pulley works

as if this were all there were to teaching. This is a most inadequate level of planning. What is required of student teachers is that they can show that they have thought about *how* this explanation is to be achieved. A mentor can legitimately ask for evidence that they have thought about different ways in which this could be done. A mentor might wish to know whether they have thought about the effectiveness of different methods given the nature of the group which they have to teach. Mentors will not mind too much if the method chosen does not work brilliantly. But they will be very concerned about a lack of any thought at all on the appropriateness of different teaching methods. A lesson plan should show the *how* in some detail, and perhaps even mention the other methods that were considered but not employed. The what, when and why of the lesson can often be generic to the course as a whole, and act as constraints upon the teacher. But the *how* is based upon professional judgements regarding the content and the pupils. It involves teachers making professional and pedagogical decisions about the quality of the learning experiences which are being created for their pupils. It is often this aspect of teaching practice which mentors want to discuss most with new teachers after they have observed their lessons.

Hitting the Right Levels

In deciding upon and planning the *how* of a lesson, an important consideration for any teacher is the specific needs and abilities of their pupils. Hitting the right levels – *differentiation* – is something which student teachers often find very difficult, and their judgements about appropriate levels of work and amounts of work are, to begin with, often far from realistic.

Many student teachers have been out of schools for a minimum of three years and, in some cases, for anything between five and 35 years. Their knowledge of schools and of schooling will be based on their own memories, which are often not the best or most appropriate guide to the current demands and practices. One cannot base judgements about current school pupils on observations and experiences which were gained in different sorts of schools, in a different educational climate, using (often) different sorts of teaching methods than are used and required today. The rural school is not a model for teaching in an urban school; a grammar school, a public school and a secondary modern school are not representative of life in a large comprehensive; a single-sex school poses different problems to a co-educational school; a traditional type of schooling is often at odds with more progressive pedagogies. The National Curriculum ensures that what is taught now is structured in a different way from that before 1990. New teachers may also find that discipline is handled differently, uniforms may have changed, and more responsibility may be given to pupils to organize their own learning than was the case in previous years. New teachers may face a vast array of differences between their own schooling and that which is to be found on teaching practice, and inevitably this is something of a culture shock.

In planning a lesson, teachers are required not to aim it at *one* level, but at the various levels of abilities and needs which make up the whole class. A lesson plan, therefore, does not aim at a right level, but at the *right levels*. Teachers can produce the most brilliant and innovative lesson plan, with superb resources, but if their pupils find the work too easy or too difficult then, either way, they are likely to lose interest, and to lose confidence in their teacher. If teachers do not hit the right levels in the work they set, then they and their pupils will not have successful lessons. Therefore student teachers on teaching practice are advised to take the opportunity to observe their groups and other teachers, and to examine pupils' previous work, so that the appropriate levels can be identified and planned for.

A lesson plan ought not only to try and repeat the success of a pupil at the same level, it must try to encourage success at the next, higher level. Outcomes have to be designed which will ensure that pupil learning is able to progress. Those outcomes must form part of a teacher's lesson planning, and should be explicit in the planning of student teachers. However, it is always necessary to begin with where the pupils are, before trying to move them on! Once the levels at which pupils can enjoy success have been recognized, then teachers can begin to raise expectations and to demand more. Encouraging a pupil to succeed at new levels works best when it is the result of a relationship of trust and confidence between teacher and pupil. That trust and confidence is itself the result of lessons which the pupils have understood and enjoyed, and in which they have already experienced success.

Reserving Judgements

It is prudent for student teachers to be cautious before making snap judgements about what they find in their schools. Their own backgrounds, their own schooling, and even their own personal politics may prove unhelpful in trying to gain a realistic insight into the standards and practices which they find. Common complaints by student teachers in their first few weeks of teaching practice are that standards of discipline are low, expectations of the pupils are low, and above all that the standard of work which pupils produce is disappointingly low.

Three sorts of comments might make appropriate responses to these snap judgements. First, it is wise to be at least suspicious of the view that things in education have got worse. There has not been a golden time in the twentieth century (or any other century) when things were so much better than they are today. If a criterion of a successful education service is that it provides educational opportunities and relative success for *all* children, then it is hard to see any time in the last 50 or even 1500 years when so many have been able to achieve so much.

Have things got worse?

Sparta, in ancient Greece:
If the child were strong, orders were given for its education. But if it were weak or deformed, it was ordered to be thrown into a deep cavern, concluding that its life would be no advantage either to itself or to the public.

(Plutarch, 1914, p.255)

Athens, in ancient Greece:
If the child yield a willing obedience, all is well; if not, they treat him like a young tree that is twisted and bent and try to straighten him with threats and blows. After this they send him to school, with a strict charge to the master to pay far greater heed to the good behaviour of their children than to their progress in reading and music.

(Plato, 1956, para.325d)

Ancient Rome:
Graffiti from Pompeii testify to boredom with school lessons, and someone at Rome made a sketch of a heavily laden donkey, with the caption: 'Toil on ass, as I have done, and much good it will profit you'.

(Bonner, 1977, p.141)

St Augustine, (AD 354–430):
I loved not study, and hated to be forced to it. Yet I was forced. ...Why then did I hate the Greek classic?...For not one word of it did I understand, and to make me understand I was urged vehemently with cruel threats and punishments.

(Augustine, 1907, pp.12, 14–15)

Cathedral schools of the Middle Ages
The boys walked, read and chanted, like brethren in religion, and whatever had to be sung at the steps of the choir or in the choir itself they sang and chanted by heart, one or two more together, without the help of a book. One boy never looked at another when they were in their places in choir, except sideways and that very seldom, and they never spoke a word to one another...

(Parry, 1920, p.42)

19th-century public schools:
In 1797 Dr. Inglis, the Headmaster of Rugby and nicknamed 'the Black Tiger' by his pupils, had his study door blown off with gunpowder and only the reading of the Riot Act and the appearance of the military forced the students into surrender. An outburst at Eton in 1818 pursuaded (even) Dr. Keate (Headmaster of Eton, 1809–1834) to vacate the premises whilst his charges took a sledgehammer to his fine oaken desk. Winchester was often hit by serious disturbances, one rising there also in 1818 required the intervention of soldiers armed with fixed bayonets before order was restored.

(Evans, 1975, p.48)

Womens' education up to 1792:
All the writers who have written on the subject of female education and manners... have contributed to render women more artificial, weak characters than they would otherwise have been; and consequently more useless members of society.

Mankind should all be educated after the same model, or the intercourse of the sexes will never deserve the name of fellowship, nor will women ever fulfil the peculiar duties of their sex, till they become enlightened citizens, till they become free by being enabled to earn their own subsistence, independent of men....

(Wollstonecraft, 1992, pp.103, p.283)

> *State education up to the 1944 Act:*
> The layout of the C19th and early C20th elementary classroom was designed on mass production lines and the school's structure itself modelled on the factory. Its not-so-hidden curriculum conditioned pupils to 'pay attention', to 'stop talking', to unquestioning obedience, to acceptance of corporal punishment, to punctuality, neatness, frugality, token rewards for hard work and other virtues which were held to be in keeping with their lowly station in life....
>
> (Richmond, 1978, pp.32–3)

Second, is it really surprising that those fresh out of industry or university, used to working at a particular level, should find the levels at which Year Seven pupils are working something of a shock, perhaps even something of a comedown? Those training to be teachers are already relatively successful in the education system, and may now be asked to work with those who are having difficulties with things which they themselves were successful with, and found straightforward. If the experience of 'comedown' is too great then one must question whether teaching is really a sensible option for that person. The point for teachers is not to criticize and disapprove of the pupils they have to teach, but practically to help those pupils to improve, to gain confidence and to succeed. A very hard professional line can be taken here. Comprehensive teachers have no choice but to accept and to begin with where their pupils are, not where they wish they were or where they think they ought to be. Hitting the right levels means hitting the *pupils'* levels, not the *teachers'*.

Third, to improve standards teachers have to ensure that their own teaching is as effective and successful for their pupils as it can be. Whether new teachers are surprised, disappointed, alarmed, cynical or whatever about what they find in schools (or delighted, as many student teachers are) they will still be required to make the same response, and that is to do the best job they can for their pupils. New teachers do the educational chances of their pupils no favours by bringing into the classroom a set of expectations which are unrealistic and inappropriate for those pupils. If they then rigidly apply these expectations, they have not even begun to think about hitting the right levels. All they have done is import a set of dogmas into their classroom which they expect (demand?) their pupils to conform to. Such an approach is unlikely to fulfil the demand that lessons are appropriate, effective and successful. The levels of work and behaviour, and the expectations which teachers can sensibly have of their pupils, cannot be imposed without reference to the people in front of them. New teachers will know when they have succeeded in preparing a lesson at the appropriate levels, because pupils will be actively engaged, interested and producing good work. At this point, the new teacher suddenly begins to experience how satisfying teaching can be.

Evaluation

The most frightening thing for new teachers can often be the knowledge that someone is coming into their lessons to watch them. Amazingly, teaching can be a very private and isolated activity. Teachers close their doors, and no one else knows quite what is going on. However, new teachers, and student teachers in particular, have a very visible classroom, and various people will want access at certain times. There is, as always, a balance to be struck here between ensuring adequate supervision and giving student teachers a degree of autonomy in their *own* classrooms and with their *own* groups.

When student teachers are being watched, they are usually aware that they are being judged. For any judgement to be possible there must be criteria against which they will be measured. It is in the interest of student teachers to make sure they have read and understood those criteria *before* anyone begins judging them against them. It is equally important to make sure that their interpretation of those criteria is shared by all those who will be using them. It can boost confidence considerably to know that everyone involved is working with the same definitions of a successful practice, and is working towards the same results.

Criteria for assessment will vary from course to course, but all will involve most of the following areas: the ability to plan and deliver work within the National Curriculum framework; the ability to offer differentiated work; good communication skills; the ability to organize and manage classrooms; the ability to form good working relationships with staff and students, and to keep good records of pupil attendance, progress and special needs.

Competences expected of newly qualified teachers.

Subject Knowledge
2.2   Newly qualified teachers should be able to demonstrate:
    2.2.1.   an understanding of the knowledge, concepts and skills of their specialist subjects and of the place of these subjects within the school curriculum;
    2.2.2.   knowledge and understanding of the national curriculum and

attainment targets (NCATs) and the programmes of study (POS) in the subjects they are preparing to teach, together with an understanding of the framework of the statutory requirements;

2.2.3. a breadth and depth of subject knowledge extending beyond POS and examination syllabuses in school.

Subject Application

2.3 Newly qualified teachers should be able to:

2.3.1. produce coherent lesson plans which take account of NCATs and of the school's curriculum policies;

2.3.2. ensure continuity and progression within and between classes and in subjects;

2.3.3. set appropriately demanding expectations for pupils;

2.3.4. employ a range of teaching strategies appropriate to the age, ability and attainment level of pupils;

2.3.5. present subject content in clear language and in a stimulating manner;

2.3.6. contribute to the development of pupils' language and communication skills;

2.3.7. demonstrate ability to select and use appropriate resources, including Information Technology.

Class Management

2.4. Newly qualified teachers should be able to:

2.4.1. decide when teaching the whole class, groups, pairs, or individuals is appropriate for particular learning purposes;

2.4.2. create and maintain a purposeful and orderly environment for the pupils;

2.4.3. devise and use appropriate rewards and sanctions to maintain an effective learning environment;

2.4.4. maintain pupils' interest and motivation.

Assessment and Recording of Pupils' Progress

2.5. Newly qualified teachers should be able to:

2.5.1. identify the current level of attainment of individual pupils using NCATs, statements of attainment and end of key stage statements where applicable;

2.5.2. judge how well each pupil performs against the standard expected of a pupil of that age;

2.5.3. assess and record systematically the progress of individual pupils;

2.5.4. use such assessment in their teaching;

2.5.5. demonstrate that they understand the importance of reporting to pupils on their progress and of marking their work regularly against agreed criteria.

Further Professional Development

2.6.   Newly qualifed teachers should have acquired in initial   teacher training the necessary foundation to develop:

2.6.1.   an understanding of the school as an institution and its place within the community;

2.6.2.   a working knowledge of their pastoral, contractual, legal and administrative responsibilities as teachers;

2.6.3.   an ability to develop effective working relationships with professional colleagues and parents, and to develop their communication skills;

2.6.4.   an awareness of individual differences, including social, psychological, developmental and cultural dimensions;

2.6.5.   the ability to recognise diversity of talent including that of gifted pupils;

2.6.6.   the ability to identify special educational needs or learning difficulties;

2.6.7.   a self-critical approach to diagnosing and evaluating pupils' learning, including a recognition of the effects on that learning of teachers' expectations;

2.6.8.   a readiness to promote the moral and spiritual well-being of pupils.

(from DfE Circular No.9/92, annex A)

Within any scheme which requires the judging of one person by another there can arise the suspicion that a hidden agenda operates. With clear and open lines of communication this need not be the case. Mentors have to bear in mind that student teachers feel very vulnerable and it is not surprising if, at times, they feel either that they are under constant surveillance or that they have to teach to please whoever is monitoring them. This can pose a difficult problem. Clearly, if the styles of established teachers and student teachers are completely at odds then disagreements may occur. But such disagreements have to be handled in a professional way. A certain level of insecurity in student teachers is understandable, but compromises have to be reached. Mentors are unwise to demand rigid conformity to a particular style of teaching. However, they have a right to expect that the style adopted is producing effective learning for (their) pupils. They have to go back in and teach the group when the student teacher has left, and are understandably cautious, therefore, about what they might find.

Perhaps the most overt aspect of any hidden agenda is noise. New teachers (and often established teachers) are very often concerned that their lessons may be judged solely on how noisy they are. Strange as it might sound, what is often important is not the amount of noise so much as the type of noise which is produced. Music and drama lessons are often *supposed* to produce noise. A technology workshop will often be very noisy indeed. It is a question of what sort of noise is appropriate for each particular lesson. Pupils working in groups excitedly passing and gathering information and ideas produce an industrious atmosphere which teachers will recognize as productive and educational. Role plays, discussions, debates, etc. often get people excited – adults as well as children – so expectations for those lessons must incorporate that. But equally, people shouting or screaming to no useful purpose, that is, in a way inappropriate to the content and plan of the lesson, is something which has to be dealt with.

Fear of a noisy classroom often prevents student teachers from trying new things, from learning about and expressing their full range of abilities, and from creating a variety of learning experiences for their pupils. This is regrettable, and often a waste of talent. Supportive, helpful and above all wise counsel from mentors can help student teachers to achieve a balance between a variety of different styles of lessons, whilst keeping the noise issue in perspective. Whether the noise in a classroom is a problem or not depends on the lesson itself and whether it forms a necessary part of the desired result. Good teachers point out to their pupils at the start of a lesson that expectations about noise may vary during the lesson depending on the activity they are engaged in. Warning pupils of these expecations in advance often makes reminding them later that much easier and more effective.

The performance of student teachers in the classroom can be judged and analysed by at least four types of people. First and probably most importantly, a student teacher's own pupils will be constantly evaluating how well their new teacher is doing – not in any formal way, but they will be observing and monitoring the newcomer until their own involvement in and enthusiasm for their learning takes their minds off this 'supervisory' role. Student teachers need not be afraid to seek their pupils' evaluations of lessons, although written rather than verbal responses prove much more manageable. This is done very often for adult learners, but is rather less common for younger pupils. It could be argued that such an approach shows teachers accepting that they are accountable to the pupils they teach, and that they are taking seriously their commitment to providing all pupils with the best possible opportunities for effective learning.

Student teachers will also be evaluated by their mentor. Their concerns will reflect the professional expectations made of all new teachers in comprehensive education, and which are the substance of this book. Critiques of lessons can often make student teachers feel that they are under attack, and force them to become defensive, which is unhelpful in seeking to move forward. It is worth bearing in mind two points. First, student teachers and mentors need to remember that the former are *student* teachers, and therefore still learning the job. They cannot be expected to put in faultless performances. Instead, they are expected to be gaining experiences and learning from mistakes. Rather than feel under attack, it is often much more productive for student teachers to listen to the criticisms, ask questions, and seek guidance for next time. No matter how well they feel they have done, there is always a criticism that can be made, and it may just be that *their* mentor seems to be the sort of person who will pick out that criticism at the expense of all the other good work.

The third party involved in evaluation is the university/college tutor. Depending on the nature of the course, they will play a greater or lesser role on teaching practice. At any event it is to be hoped that they can be used to express any concerns which, for any reason, student teachers feel unable to share with their mentors in school. However, sometimes the system works the other way round and a good relationship with a mentor enables the student to discuss problems about the course (and its personnel) with them. It is a skill not only in teaching but in all employment to be able to judge whom one feels one can trust, and in whom to confide. But people who are ultimately responsible for passing or failing students may wish to keep the relationship at a distance, and confidants may need to be others who have a less formal responsibility for supervising the teaching practice. As the supervisory role increasingly moves from college to school, students may not see anyone from the college at all on their teaching practice.

Finally, student teachers must evaluate their own performance. Good teachers do this almost as second nature. As they get to know their job and their pupils they cannot help but constantly monitor what worked well, what didn't work well, who succeeds at which type of work, what sorts of lessons they themselves prefer and enjoy most success with. Ask teachers how much evaluation they undertake and they will probably give an embarrassed grin and say 'not enough'. Yet listen to their conversations in the staffroom or the office when they are talking about groups or individuals, and one can often hear that evaluation has become instinctive to them. However, student teachers have to make their evaluations very deliberate and highly visible.

To begin with, student teachers need to try to evaluate each of their lessons. It is good practice to measure performance against the agreed course criteria mentioned above. Then, as knowledge is gained of each teaching group, they will also be able to evaluate the progress of their pupils, and the suitability of particular types and levels of work for them.

Evaluation is not an end in itself. The point of self-evaluation is to try and ensure that one becomes a more effective teacher, constantly improving the effectiveness of pupil learning. Evaluation is a means to the end of becoming an effective practitioner in whom pupils can have confidence because they know that they will enjoy success.

It is very noticeable that, as student teachers improve, their comments on lessons move on from general comments about the group, for example, 'this group is very noisy', 'this group is full of troublemakers', 'this group is lazy', to more specific comments about the learning needs of particular pupils or groups of pupils. This is good professional development. Student teachers ought, as soon as possible, to move on from the evaluation of a group as one homogeneous lump to a more sophisticated analysis of the individuals and characters who constitute the group. This enables teachers to begin to respond to their pupils' individual needs, and therefore to increase their pupils' chances of successful learning.

Inevitably the 'characters' in the class draw a teacher's attention first, but this should only serve to remind the teacher also to get to know those pupils who say little or nothing. Evaluations of lessons can be helpful in making notes on individuals and in shaping thoughts about the particular needs of each pupil. No one is suggesting that by the end of a teaching practice student teachers will know every pupil or be successful with all of them. Far from it. That is an unrealistic expectation to have of any student teacher. But it needs to be realized that evaluation is not something student teachers need to do only because the course requires it. Self-evaluation by all teachers is a professional requirement because it is one of the means to achieving more effective teaching and, thus, more successful learning for their pupils.

CHAPTER TWO

Relationships

Teachers have to establish professional working relationships with a wide variety of people, both within schools and outside. This chapter describes the nature of some of those relationships, and looks in particular at the expectations placed upon student teachers in this regard.

With Pupils

On the pupil–teacher relationship

Teachers should no longer induce in children a feeling of subjection and bondage – to make them obey another's will even in unimportant matters – to demand absolute obedience for obedience's sake, and by severity to obtain what really belongs alone to the feelings of love and reverence....
A society of students cannot be regarded as an assemblage of servants, nor should they have the appearance or behaviour of such. Education to independence demands that young people should be accumstomed early to consult their own sense of propriety and their own reason.

(Hegel, from Mackenzie, 1909, pp.174–5)

My midwifery has all the standard features, except that I practise it on men instead of women, and supervise the labour of their minds, not their bodies. And the most important aspect of my skill, is the ability to apply every conceivable test to see whether the young man's mental offspring is illusory and false or viable and true. But I have *this* feature in common with midwives – I am myself barren of wisdom.

(Socrates, from Plato, 1987, para.150c)

Let the teacher above all things adopt the attitude of parent towards his pupils and consider that he is taking the place of those who entrust their children to him....

In correcting faults he will not be harsh and never abusive; for many are driven away from the studies they have entered upon by the fact that some teachers find fault as though they hated the offender...

For as it is the duty of the one to teach, so it is the duty of these others to prove themselves apt to learn: otherwise neither is sufficient without the other.

(Quintilian in Smail, 1938, pp.73, 74, 105)

Respect for the pupil is just as important as respect for the teacher, because after a young person's opinion has been disregarded three or four times the young person may never express an opinion again.

(Blishen, 1969, p.143)

A careful analysis of the teacher-student relationship at any level, inside or outside the school, reveals its fundamentally *narrative* character. This relationship involves a narrating Subject (the teacher) and patient, listening objects (the students).... Education is suffering from narration sickness....

Narration turns them (the students) into 'containers', into receptacles to be filled by the teacher. The more completely he fills the receptacles, the better a teacher he is. The more meekly the receptacles permit themselves to be filled, the better students they are.

(Freire, 1972, p.45)

The outcome of these two distinctive characteristics of teacher-pupil interaction is the great inequality of the two participants in the process of defining the situation. The dice are loaded in the teacher's favour. He can take the initiative in defining the situation and possesses the power to enforce it on the pupils.

(Hargreaves, 1975, p.115)

Equal value

Teacher/pupil relationships are shaped by styles of teaching and learning, and by the personalities of the participants. However, the character and nature of comprehensive education also imposes certain professional expectations on the relationship. A basic principle of comprehensive education is that it recognizes the pupils' unconditional entitlement to a state-funded education, regardless of their race, gender and social background. Equally, pupils' abilities, attitudes, motivations and personalities are not formal barriers against which that entitlement becomes conditional. Pupils do not have to fulfil any list of desirable characteristics in order to receive this entitlement. It is theirs by right no matter who they are, no matter what their strengths and weaknesses, and no matter what their levels of motivation. Since no 'type' of child is, *in principle,* favoured or valued more highly than any other, the education of all children in comprehensive education is held to be of equal value.

The comprehensive teacher is faced with the enormous challenge of turning this comprehensive principle into classroom practice. Different schools will treat this challenge more or less seriously. Nevertheless, the new teacher, in fulfilling his or her comprehensive responsibilities, needs to try and respond positively to this challenge, and one of the most fundamental ways in which the comprehensive principle becomes classroom reality is through the teacher/pupil relationship. Just as the principle of comprehensive education actively *approves* of the entitlement to education of all pupils, so teachers are required to *approve* of their own particular pupils. Because the education of all children is recognized as being of equal value, every pupil can expect their own particular needs, strengths and weaknesses to be recognized and addressed. Also, they are entitled to have learning outcomes devised for them in which they will enjoy success and make progress, and to have those successes valued by teachers equally with those of other pupils.

Equal value, then, gives a concrete form to the professional demands made on teachers in respect of their relationships with pupils. It expresses the responsibility on teachers not to select one 'type' of pupil, or one programme of study, as of higher worth than another. It challenges the teacher to see the value of an educational programme in terms of its effectiveness in meeting particular needs and in developing and encouraging new and more advanced needs. Teachers are expected to have *comprehensive expectations* of and about the pupils they will be asked to teach, and not to have predetermined or selective expectations about who they might wish to teach. Selective schools have predetermined criteria about entitlement. Comprehensive schools, and therefore comprehensive teachers cannot. The opposite of a relationship based on equal value is one where some pupils are favoured over others, where the education of some is seen in principle to be more worthwhile than others, and where success, praise and value are used to discriminate in favour of some pupils and against others.

An equal value teacher/pupil relationship is therefore based on approval for the pupil simply because they are there. Such a relationship will seek to avoid anything which humiliates or degrades, and will not employ sarcasm or the public 'put down' as legitimate expressions of itself, either directly to the pupil or in their absence. The professional obligation in comprehensive education to value each pupil equally needs to be visible in all aspects of practice, both in the classroom and outside.

In sum, a teacher/pupil relationship is not wholly dependent upon nor defined by the personalities involved. Its substance is determined by the principle of comprehensive education that entitlement to education is universal. The relationship can be more or less formal – that is a matter of personal style – but it has no room for resentment or cynicism about pupils. Nor does it require the teacher to judge the relative value of one pupil against another, but rather to teach in order that all may experience success and recognize that their particular educational needs are valued (the difficulties which this presents are examined in more detail in Chapter 4). This is the professional challenge which comprehensive entitlement education sets for the teacher/pupil relationship and, in turn, for all new teachers.

Establishing the relationship

Student teachers may already have had experience forming working relationships with adults, and will almost certainly have established a 'relationship' with their subject specialism. What is far less certain is whether they will ever have had to establish working relationships with comprehensive school pupils. This is often an area of anxiety and uncertainty for student teachers. It can be very unnerving for them, in the first few weeks of their training course, to meet other students who have already helped out for four weeks in their local secondary school, or are a scout/guide leader, or whose partners are teachers, or who have 'done' Camp America, or who in some other way sound as if they already know how to work with young people.

However, such experience is not always an advantage, and indeed a lack of such experience can, in some cases, prove helpful in preparing for teaching practice. People who have 'worked with children' are not always best placed to enter the comprehensive school with the open mind referred to in Chapter 1. They can, all too easily, measure the pupils they are given to teach according to expectations produced and gained with other young people. These expectations may not, therefore, be realistic or appropriate for their classes. New teachers who enter the comprehensive classroom without such preconceptions are often better placed to allow the class and the pupils to 'speak for themselves'. They are often more easily able to accommodate the comprehensive range of ability, attitude and personality they find in their lessons, as this variety does not run counter to what they expected (or hoped) to find there. Schools and mentors welcome student teachers who have come to learn about the requirements of comprehensive education more than they do student teachers who think they already know about them.

24

> **Real pupils**
>
> With a tightening of the stomach I realise that teaching practice begins very soon now. We have scarcely met any real live children. In fact only one or two visits to a comprehensive school in the East End. My chief memory of these is of the group trouping into the school building to the cockney jeers of some second formers. One counted us off with extravagant gestures, 'stu-dent, stu-dent, stu-dent', and with that falling mocking cadence children use to taunt.
>
> (Otty, 1972, p.19)

Just as new teachers have to form professional working relationships with staff, so do they with their pupils. But establishing relationships with pupils is not necessarily a two-way process, at least to begin with, and does not require mutual action by both parties. A class of pupils faced with a new teacher can wait and see what the new teacher is like before they have to commit themselves to any relationship. This is the so-called 'honeymoon period'. The teacher, however, is afforded no such luxuries. She (or he) has to perform, to commit herself to establishing a relationship, as soon as she walks in. It is the teacher who has to make the first moves in establishing a relationship, and the pupils' judgements of those first moves often determine the sort of relationship which the teacher and the group will have *after* the honeymoon!

Therefore, the way in which student teachers and their classes are introduced to each other is crucial to the sort of relationships which will be established. Mentors and colleagues have the responsibility for those sorts of decisions, but there tend to be two distinct approaches: 'the deep end' and 'the drip feed'.

The deep end

This describes the approach where student teachers are simply put in front of a new class, armed with their lesson plan and resources, and told to get on with it. It is a 'sink or swim' approach, favoured by teachers who see effective teaching in terms of control and survival. However, it is often the approach favoured by student teachers themselves, particularly at the beginning of their practice, because the thing they really want to know is, 'Can I do it?' This simplistic question reflects their anxieties about classroom control, but it does not reflect careful thought or consideration about what exactly a teacher does, nor about what constitutes successful and effective teaching. It is also the approach which is most likely to expose student teachers to situations which they are ill-prepared to deal with. Most important, it is an approach which dismisses the importance of flexible and responsive teacher/pupil relationships in the classroom. It assumes that no other relationship is required than that of control by the teacher over the pupils, regardless of who those pupils are, or their specific needs.

The drip feed

This approach reflects a much more considered method of establishing relationships between student teachers and their pupils. It often takes the form of a stepped programme where contact between the two is established gradually over a period of time. A common pattern is for student teachers to begin by sitting in on some lessons which are taken by the usual class teacher, then to get to know some of the pupils by moving around the room and offering help and support with the work. The class teacher may then feel that the student can be given a small group of pupils to work with for a while, or perhaps to team-teach a few lessons where the teacher begins and ends the lesson, and the student organizes an activity in the middle. The stage at which the teacher leaves the student alone in the classroom can be discussed or, more often, a teacher simply 'leaves' for a few minutes to get the pupils used to having only the student in the classroom. Mentors can ensure that student teachers are 'in charge' of a class long before the students realize it themselves. Such an approach is slow, but allows confidence to be gained at each step, and for students to build on successes. The important skills of beginning and ending lessons can again be practised through team-teaching, where the class teacher can play a greater or lesser role as required, before full responsibility for lessons is given over to students. What this approach takes seriously is that the relationship between teacher and pupil is important, and has to be very carefully nurtured, developed and shaped if it is to respond to the needs of all who are involved: student, pupil and teacher.

Confidentiality

The professional requirements of the teacher/pupil relationship are particularly clear regarding the issue of confidentiality. Teachers are *not* in a position to offer a pupil confidentiality. If a pupil offers to tell the teacher something provided that the teacher promises not to tell anyone else, the teacher cannot agree to this. Apart from the fact that the teacher does not know what the pupil is about to say, and cannot therefore predict in advance what the nature of the information may be, it is also likely that the teacher will be required professionally or by law to tell at least one other person about the conversation with the pupil. It would therefore be dishonest to pretend to a pupil that the matter will go no further. The teachers' professional responsibility is to do the best thing in such circumstances for their pupils. But exactly what the best thing is in any particular case is seldom straightforward. To discuss the issue with other colleagues may often be in the interests of the teacher as well as those of the pupil.

> Department for Education Circular 5/94 states that it is 'inappropriate' for teachers to give individual advice to students about sexual matters, as teachers should not encroach upon parental rights and responsibilities. If it appears that the law about sexual intercourse is being broken, the teacher should consult the Head so that appropriate counselling can be arranged.
>
> *(TES,* 1994a)

A pupil seeking out a teacher in order to share something with him or her deserves compassion and concern, but with that must also come the courage to be straight with them from the start. If a pupil has seen fit to trust a teacher, the teacher must reflect that trust, and offer honesty and openness from the beginning. If confidentiality is the pre-requisite for pupils disclosing their information, then a teacher cannot accept. But experienced teachers will have ways of explaining the difficulties of their position to the pupil. They will make it absolutely clear that they do want to hear what the pupil has to say and to help if possible, but that it may be necessary for them to tell someone else. Teachers will explain to the pupil that they cannot offer confidentiality, but in such a way as to present this as help and support, and not as disloyalty, or as an abuse of the confidentiality which the pupil is seeking from them. If the teacher/pupil relationship embodies a mutual respect for, and valuing of each other, then it will survive this explanation about confidentiality, and may well be stronger for it.

Student teachers do not always have the experience required to deal with such situations professionally. Yet they are often just the people that some pupils will single out as sympathetic, seeing them as not yet part of 'the system', or often as 'easier to talk to'. This may be flattering, but the same guidelines apply to student teachers, and confidentiality should not be offered, even if the result of that appears to the pupil to be a rejection.

Allied to this issue is the concern that many teachers are increasingly coming to share, that teachers and student teachers should not engineer, or be engineered into being alone in a room with a pupil of the opposite sex. Again, it is the case that student teachers can become the objects of attention from pupils, either out of genuine curiosity, or perhaps a somewhat more mischievous interest. But more serious are attentions from pupils which might be seen as flirtatious, or even as a form of harassment. Student teachers need to develop very quickly an awareness for when the attentions of pupils become less than comfortable for them, and equally quickly how to deal with this. Sometimes it is the case that the best thing to do is to ignore it. The teacher neither acknowledges it, nor accuses anyone of doing it, perhaps not even letting the pupil know that he or she is aware of it. Starved of recognition from the teacher, such attentions can quickly fade away. However, if the student teacher feels that it is becoming a problem, then, at the very least, they must tell someone about it, seek advice, and keep a colleague or mentor informed. If the student teacher is going to be in a situation in which there may be some uncertainty – for example, help with work after school – then they can ensure that other people are always around, and perhaps arrange for another member of staff to be in the room with them.

Confidentiality, pupil flirtations and harassment may seem strange subjects to be included in a book for the new teacher. Whilst they may not be relevant to everyone's experience as a teacher, nor to most student teachers on teaching practice, for the few that they do affect, it can be a most serious and occasionally damaging situation if handled inappropriately. To be able actively to avoid the misunderstandings and ambiguities which such situations produce *before* they arise is also part of a teacher's professional responsibilities and skills, and therefore something to be prepared for in advance.

With Staff

Professional relationships

Whatever the relationship a teacher may establish with the pupils, however much contact there may be with caretakers, parents, advisors and others, his condition of life will be affected mainly by those with whom he shares the staffroom, for that is where he will find the most abiding community and conflict.

(Watts, 1974, pp.27-8)

It is important that the diversity of teachers succeeding each other prevent the influence of anyone from being too exclusive and therefore too restrictive to the individuality of the child....

It is especially the principal of the school who must ensure this continuity.... He must put the teachers in contact with each other to prevent them from acting autonomously rather than in concert.

(Durkheim, 1973, pp.247–8)

General expectations

In any institution it is rare for people to be able to choose who they work with. Student teachers have little or no choice at all. Just as for established teachers, there is a requirement on NQTs and student teachers that they form 'working relationships' with colleagues. Such relationships can make many, often difficult demands of teachers, and particularly of new teachers. They require teachers to be able to work together in producing, teaching and evaluating courses, to discuss and agree upon policies, both departmental and whole-school, and to offer support, guidance and appraisal where appropriate. For some teachers, professionalism in working relationships means, above all else, that they are backed up by colleagues if and when required. In forming working relationships it is not necessary for teachers to particularly like their colleagues, although whatever their personal feelings about those with whom they work, they share the collective responsibility which all teachers have, to provide their pupils with appropriate, effective and successful learning.

For student teachers there are some important guidelines to observe in establishing and maintaining successful and professional relationships with staff. A seemingly trivial point is that it does help to be prepared to talk to people. Saying 'Good morning' is noticed and appreciated. People do not want to work with gloomy, grumpy souls who seldom talk or join in. It is expected of student teachers that they will make the effort to get on with people, and if staff see them making this effort they will respond. It is often surprising how much is forgiven in lack of technique if student teachers are seen to be keen, to work hard, to be enthusiastic, to listen to advice and ask for help.

On occasions, there are personality clashes between mentors and student teachers. These are difficult to resolve and have to be handled very carefully by all concerned. The first priority in such a situation is to ensure that the clash does not affect the judgements made upon the abilities and competences of the students. The latter should be able to expect that the professionalism of their mentors ensures that this is so. It is worth remembering that a problem with one colleague is not also a problem with the whole department or the whole school, and students should be able to demonstrate good relationships with staff other than their mentor. However, student teachers will not be thanked for moaning about one member of staff to another. That is a 'privilege' reserved for full-time members of staff and wholly inappropriate for student teachers. A liaison tutor, who is more detached from the school may well be the appropriate sounding-board for these sorts of concerns.

It is important for student teachers to try to get involved in anything which the school is engaged in outside of the formal curriculum. At the very least they should attend departmental or staff meetings. Student teachers who always leave for home on the bell (as they say) can easily give a bad impression, and are denied the opportunity to sit and chat with colleagues after school, even if only for a short time. If there is an important reason to leave, for example, picking up children after school, then it is in the students' own interests to ensure that their colleagues know and understand this.

If student teachers get the opportunity, or can make the opportunity to attend any after-school activities or productions, or to go on visits, then this is highly recommended. It is not only a visible sign of interest, enthusiasm and commitment, it also enables them to get to know staff and pupils away from the pressures of lessons and of the institution in general. Students might find a particular area of activity which interests them and be able to give this some of their time. This, too, is very favourably received, and forms part of the judgements which are made about them as a possible teacher.

Student teachers ought not to talk about other staff to their pupils, even if (or especially if) their pupils are encouraging them to do so, nor seek pupil opinion about other staff. Any comments passed on to pupils about other staff can be relayed and amended through the grapevine back to the person concerned, and eventually the source of the information will be in some trouble. Talking about other teachers in front of pupils is simply unprofessional whether it comes from teachers or pupils. In return, student teachers can expect support from their colleagues if and when they make mistakes in their dealings with pupils. The support and advice of colleagues in such situations is vital for student teachers and, handled in a professional way, should enable them to return to the pupil or group with whom the problem arose and continue teaching them. Depending on the school and the department, student teachers may be asked to try and put the situation right themselves by, for example, discussing the problem with the pupil(s) concerned. Some teachers will prefer to deal with such things themselves, although to do so can deny students an important opportunity to gain valuable experience. Whatever the method employed, student teachers can expect colleagues not to embarrass or compromise them in front of their classes.

Just as it is unprofessional to undermine colleagues in front of pupils, so there are professional expectations with regard to how staff talk about pupils to each other. It is a common experience for student teachers to be shocked and disheartened by the way some teachers talk about pupils in the privacy of the staffroom or the office. Student teachers are often very aware of the need to avoid labelling and self-fulfilling prophecies when they begin their training, but then find that for some teachers labelling is a much enjoyed sport.

Talking about pupils

...The characteristics of the pupils referred to in the staffroom represent obstacles to be recognised, not problems that can be solved by the adoption of appropriate methods. In fact the explanations for pupil behaviour implied in Downtown teachers' typifications of their pupils are not strictly speaking explanations at all, they have the form of predictions and function as excuses. They specify dangers and limits involved in teaching Downtown pupils, rather than being concerned with identifying problems and finding strategies for solving them.

P –   O'Brien is in the top set for Maths.

B –   Has O'Brien got anything upstairs?

P –   No, neither has (name), he got an E in the test, oh 'n' then a B I think.

T –   He doesn't even know his three times table.

T –   Most of them don't.

W –   (Name), he's so lazy, it takes him twenty minutes to pick up the pencil and twenty minutes to put it down. (Name) looks prehistoric, I wonder if he's on drugs.

(from Hargreaves and Woods, 1984, pp.212, 209, 213–4)

If the teacher regards the child as inferior because (for example) he is a liar, if he despises or dislikes the child for this, then, whatever else we may think about the rightness and wrongness of this response, one thing is certain: the attitude will impede the teacher from obeying the comprehensive principle in relation to the child. I do not think it would make sense to say, 'My contempt for this child does not in any serious way prevent me from practising the principle that his education is of equal value to that of other children.'

(Daunt, 1975, p.89)

In line with the obligation on teachers to value equally the educational needs, abilities, strengths and weaknesses of all pupils, it is clearly unprofessional for teachers to belittle any pupil on grounds of ability. However, if staffroom talk, or the jokes of departmental colleagues include such a lack of professionalism, student teachers can find themselves caught between competing demands. On the one hand, they do not wish to be part of such conversations, nor do they wish to hear pupils talked about in that way. On the other hand, they realize the need to get on with people and to join in wherever possible. This tension for student teachers between adhering to their own professional standards and risking being judged as idealistic and/or aloof, or joining in and thus compromising their own educational ideals, can be one of their toughest initiation rituals. What is often worse is the hypocrisy of some teachers who, whilst using derogatory labels themselves, do not approve of student teachers doing so. Nor are such teachers particularly impressed with student teachers who challenge them about such issues.

The mentor

Lastly, one of the greatest strains in making relationships with staff can often be produced by the fact that, at some point, teachers, and mentors in particular, have to assess whether student teachers have passed or failed their teaching practice. Formal assessment is a pressure on both the assessor and the assessed. Part of the working relationship, therefore, which has to be established between mentors and students, must be a clear and shared perception of what is expected, what is being asked for, and what criteria will be used to form judgements about success and failure. Very open lines of communication are vital here, and it is good practice early on for both to sit down together and establish exactly what those expectations are.

There will be a set of competences which a mentor is working with, and student teachers should have a copy of these. However, every mentor and every school may have a different emphasis about what constitutes successful teaching practice. For some, a student teacher's relationships with other staff may be paramount; for others, a student's relationships with pupils. Some may feel that lesson planning and preparation have the highest priority; others may concentrate more on actual classroom performance. Whatever the particular priorities are, it is in the interest of student teachers to ensure that they are spelled out, so that they can have an insight into the priorities of their assessor. The worst situation of all arises *either* when mentors announce late in the practice that students have not been doing something which they should have done, when they did not actually realize that it was expected, *or,* when a mentor fails to alert students early enough in the practice that there are weaknesses in certain areas of their practice which will have to be addressed. In these cases, mentors have a responsibility to work on these areas with students, and the relationship should be such that clear advice can be given and then acted upon. Student teachers cannot be allowed to believe they are doing satisfactorily if they are not. Neither should they simply be informed at the end of their practice that they have failed. Weaknesses and problems need to be identified early in the practice, and some plan of action devised to respond to those areas of weakness.

With the responsibility for initial teacher training moving increasingly away from universities and colleges and into schools, the importance of the relationship between mentor and the new teacher cannot be overestimated. It needs, above all, to be a professional working relationship.

CHAPTER THREE

Pedagogy

What is pedagogy?

Pedagogy: the art or science of teaching; instruction, discipline, training.
    Pedagogue: Latin *paedagogus,* Greek *paidagogos,* a trainer and teacher of boys.

(Oxford English Dictionary)

Paedagogue means merely the slave who had charge of bringing his master's sons safely to and from school, and guarding them from mischief by the way. He was often old and trusty, often old and useless, always ignorant and never respected.

(Mahaffey, 1881, p.29)

It was he who helped parents to instil into the children what was right and what was wrong, and all the details of proper behaviour... Among well regulated families.... the 'pedagogue' was a respected figure... generally the pedagogue appears to have been a sturdy fellow, as he needed to be, and though prone to err on the side of severity rather than leniency, often concealed a kind heart under a rough exterior.

(Bonner, 1977, p.38)

'Pedagogy' is most often defined as 'the science of teaching'. It derives from the name given to the slaves in ancient Greece who used to take the sons of their owners to school and who, in some cases, were themselves given teaching responsibilities. However, in current teacher training, and in education in general, the term 'pedagogy' is not often heard or discussed, and as a concept it has lost much of its former importance.

Its scientific credentials over the last 300 years have been based in psychology, and in particular in the 'laws' of child development and the mind. A knowledge of these 'laws', it was thought, could give rise to methods of teaching which perfectly complemented human development. If the mind at birth was a clean slate, then teaching need only consist of fixing the right images upon it. This gave rise to the science of 'didactic' teaching. If, however, the mind contained individual characteristics of its own, then teaching should simply allow it to develop according to itself. This gave rise to the science of 'child-centred education'.

Method

The art of teaching, therefore, demands nothing more than the skillful arrangement of time, of the subjects taught, and of the method. As soon as we have succeeded in finding a proper method it will be no harder to teach school-boys, in any number desired, than with the help of the printing press to cover a thousand sheets daily with the neatest writing.... It will be as pleasant to see education carried out on my plan as to look at an automatic machine of this kind, and the process will be as free from failure as are these mechanical contrivances, when skillfully made....

(Comenius, 1910, pp.96–7, written c. 1632)

For several years I have done battle for an idea concerning the instruction of man... My idea was, that in order to establish natural, rational methods, it was essential that we make numerous, exact and rational observations of man as an individual, principally during infancy....

The seat, the foot-rest, the desks are all arranged in such a way that the child can never stand at his work. He is alloted only sufficient space for sitting in an erect position. It is in such ways that schoolroom desks and benches have advanced towards perfection, every cult of the so-called scientific pedagogy has designed a model of the scientific desk.

(Montessori, 1920, pp.3 and 17)

Both methods claimed to be scientific and to be genuinely 'the science of teaching'. But the problem with any all-embracing, scientific method is that, in being prescriptive, it has decided what needs to be done *before* a judgement can be made as to its suitability. Teachers, on the other hand, in meeting their comprehensive obligations, have to make judgements about the suitability of different methods in the light of the groups and individuals who face them. Whilst the methods may be scientific, teachers' pedagogy *begins* with something else. It begins with their professional judgements about the needs and abilities of their pupils and the demands of the curriculum. The method(s) chosen are the *result* of such judgements. They are chosen according to the pupils and the curriculum, not decided upon in advance and in spite of them.

There is, therefore, an urgent need for the profession to reclaim and redefine pedagogy for itself, in a way which reflects its modern and its comprehensive responsibilities, and which is relevant to what teachers actually do. A notion of pedagogy as the science of teaching, where this refers only to one method of teaching, is no longer acceptable or relevant. It is overdeterministic, overly prescriptive, and does not reflect the actual responsibilities which comprehensive teachers have. Unwilling to select types of pupils for whom a single pedagogical method might be appropriate, comprehensive teachers accept all 'types' of pupils on an equal basis.

Pedagogy is not just a method. It is first and foremost the judgements made about which methods, given a comprehensive intake, will most effectively fulfil the aim of universal entitlement which underpins the comprehensive system. Pedagogical judgements, therefore, are grounded in the professional responsibilities and obligations which comprehensive education places upon its teachers. The judgements result in methods of teaching being adopted which bring together the pupil and the curriculum in the way(s) which are most appropriate and relevant for those particular pupils and that particular content or material.

Pedagogy, understood as this *mediation* between pupil and content, unites professional and pedagogical judgements in the one overriding obligation to ensure effective access for all to educational success. It moves the profession away from the idea that good or bad teaching can be methodologically predetermined regardless of who it is aimed at. It ensures that the *how* of teaching is the *result* of judgements concerning the *what* and the *who,* rather than a presupposition of method made regardless of them.

Pedagogy, then, mediates between learner and what is to be learnt. Each acts as a constraint upon what is possible and what is appropriate for teachers. Teachers therefore find themselves in the middle between the two sides and, with experience, they learn to accept the limitations of this position. They learn that *intervention* between pupil and content is the substance of their job. They learn that pupil and content are brought together through the teacher, and they learn that the pedagogical judgements which teachers make are themselves informed, limited, and wholly related to the needs of the pupils and the demands of the curriculum. The activity of teaching, which mediates between pupil and content, is itself mediated *by* them. Learning to accept this relationship means learning to work from the middle in the interests of both sides, and is the teacher's own continuing professional, ethical and pedagogical education.

Before examining this in more detail for the new teacher, it is useful to describe briefly the two major forms of pedagogical method which are so often opposed to each other, and which tend to dominate and even define pedagogical discussions.

35

Didactic teaching

In the history of European education, the didactic method of teaching has been the most common form of practice. The main characteristic of didactic teaching is that it seeks to *instruct* the pupil in a particular body of knowledge. This process of instruction is usually one way, from the teacher to the pupil. It usually involves the pupil in little more than passive reception of information delivered by the teacher. The authority of the teacher or the content is rarely open to question or criticism. It is a very teacher-centred and subject-centred method of teaching.

Terms which describe this sort of approach emphasize the one-sided nature of the educational relationship between teacher and pupil. For example, a didactic teacher *delivers* content, *transmits* information, *instructs* pupils, *trains* pupils, *directs* or *informs* them, even *commands* them. In the history of didactic education, the most common forms of pupil activity have been memorization, copying, reciting, listening and rehearsed disputations. These forms of 'learning' were used first in the grammar schools of the Roman Empire, adopted even more severely in the Middle Ages by religious orders, passed back from them to the church schools and grammar schools of the Renaissance and Reformation periods, and given a scientific and psychological grounding in the 17th century by, among others, Locke and Comenius. In England this approach was retained in the elementary schools of the 19th century, and in some grammar and secondary modern schools of the 20th century. It is still the favoured method of teaching of some teachers and of some schools, although the demands of comprehensive education have highlighted its weaknesses in responding to the learning needs and requirements of all pupils.

> The art of printing involves certain materials and processes. The materials consist of the paper, the type, the ink and the press. The processes consist of the preparation of the paper, the setting up and inking of the type, the correction of the proof, and the impression and drying of the copies.... [In education] instead of paper we have pupils whose minds have to be impressed with the symbols of knowledge. Instead of type, we have the class-books and the rest of the apparatus devised to facilitate the operation of teaching. The ink is replaced by the voice of the master, since it is that which conveys information from the books to the minds of the listeners; while the press is school discipline, which keeps the pupils up to their work and compels them to learn.
>
> (Comenius, 1910, p.289)

[The District School Councillor's] only concept of educating the young is the misery of endless inculcating, reprimanding, memorising – not even learning by heart but merely the misery of endless repetition, pressure and stupefaction, ceaseless spoon-feeding and stuffing. He cannot comprehend that in learning a young mind must in fact behave independently.

(Hegel, 1984, p.199)

The traditional scheme is, in essence, one of imposition from above and outside. It imposes adult standards, subject matter, and methods upon those who are only growing slowly to maturity... Learning here means acquisition of what is already incorporated in books, and in the heads of the elders.

(Dewey, 1963, pp.18–19)

Since the subject-matter as well as standards of proper conduct are handed down from the past, the attitude of pupils must, upon the whole, be one of docility, receptivity, and obedience. Books, especially text-books, are the chief representatives of the lore and wisdom of the past, while teachers are the organs through which pupils are brought into effective connection with the material. Teachers are the agents through which knowledge and skills are communicated and the rules of conduct enforced.

(Dewey, 1963, p.18)

The university or college lecture is perhaps the most common form of didactic teaching to be found in the modern education system. In some ways, this is perhaps not so surprising. Students in higher education have chosen to study a particular subject or subjects to degree level and have committed themselves to reading and researching. Lecturers, who have already passed through that particular phase of study, can expect to be able to deliver the fruits of those labours to those who come after them. Put bluntly, why should a lecturer be interested to hear student opinion until and unless that opinion is well read, well researched and informed? Aside from which, the lecture is also the most economically efficient method of transmitting information to large numbers of people.

If the teacher happens to be a man of sense, it must be an unpleasant thing to him to be conscious, while he is lecturing his students, that he is either speaking or reading nonsense, or what is very little better than nonsense. It must, too, be unpleasant to him to observe that the greater part of his students desert his lectures, or perhaps attend upon them with plain enough marks of neglect, contempt and derision.... The discipline of colleges and universities is in general contrived, not for the benefit of the students, but for the interest, or more properly speaking, for the ease of the masters. Its object is, in all cases, to maintain the authority of the master, and whether he neglects or performs his duty, to oblige the students in all cases to behave to him as if he performed it with the greatest diligence and ability.

(Smith, 1977, pp.248–9)

This didactic approach in higher education poses particular ironies for student teachers. Higher education often gives little thought or attention to its own pedagogical obligations. Indeed, many lecturers would not see themselves as teachers and therefore not accountable to the same pedagogical responsibilities as school teachers. Student teachers often find themselves being taught about the right ways to teach by lecturers whose own methods are contrary to and in opposition to the very advice which is being given.

Criticisms of this contradiction in theory and practice are common amongst student teachers. But the experience can be very useful in highlighting the professional requirements asked of teachers but not necessarily of lecturers. Pupils in schools have no choice but to attend lessons, and they are not going to display the same degree of tolerance to a boring teacher that undergraduates so often show in tedious lectures. Ultimately, undergraduates can vote with their feet; school pupils cannot. Also, school teachers cannot expect their pupils to spend hours in the library reading around the subject. Pupils will most likely return to their next lesson no better informed than when they left the previous one.

There is little to be gained by student teachers looking to their lecturers for role models of good practice. Unlike lecturers, the job of a teacher involves motivating pupils, arousing their interest and enthusiasm – not just for one subject but for learning itself – giving them exciting and stimulating work, attending to their welfare when required, developing their personal qualities, helping and supporting them when appropriate, encouraging their progress, ensuring that their work is set at appropriate levels and that material is taught in a way which responds to the needs of the pupils, and taking an interest in their many and varied non-academic achievements and talents. The list is both daunting and seemingly endless. Lecturers do not *have* to take responsibility for any of these. But for teachers, such considerations form part of their overall professional responsibilities and commitments.

For these reasons, the didactic method of teaching may no longer be the most appropriate method to employ in comprehensive education. Student teachers need to be careful not to assume that the methods found in higher education are transferable to schools. The factors upon which pedagogical decisions are based differ greatly in the two sectors. Whilst higher education seems inevitably to sway the pedagogical balance in favour of content, teachers, committed to valuing the education of all pupils equally, may need to give greater weight to the needs and interests of their pupils.

Experiential and Child-centred Learning

Experiential learning, or learning for oneself through personal experience, has an historical pedigree at least as long as that of the didactic method. Ancient Greece saw the development of the Socratic method of education where the truth of a case emerged out of a dialogue rather than a monologue, and where there was activity for both the teacher and the pupil, not just the teacher. This experiential form of teaching and learning disappeared through the Dark and Middle Ages and was only rediscovered in the Enlightenment period of European history by educationists such as Rousseau, Pestalozzi and Froebel, under the guise of child-centred learning. For these teachers, the process of learning was something done *by* the pupil, not *for them*, and should involve the use of the pupils' own senses when very young, and powers of rational and critical analysis when older. In the age of science and experimentation, when the only proof which satisfied was that which could be directly observed for oneself, it was deemed no longer sufficient for education to continue to deny direct experience as the key tool for learning.

Experiential and child-centred learning have important implications for student teachers making their pedagogical judgements on how to bring together pupil and content. They can be set against the didactic method as something which enables pupils to become active participants in their own learning, rather than simply having to rely on the teacher as the 'authority' for their information. Not surprisingly, such an approach is often popular with pupils. It can relieve the tedium of listening to teachers who are less interesting than they believe themselves to be. In some cases, it gives up the control over the material which the teacher has, and allows the pupils direct access to that knowledge and to the world.

> Do not forget it is rarely your business to suggest what he [the child] ought to learn; it is for him to want to learn, to seek and to find it. You should put it within his reach, you should skillfully awaken the desire and supply him with the means for its satisfaction.
>
> Let him know nothing because you have told him, but because he has learnt it himself. Let him not be taught science, let him discover it. If ever you substitute authority for reason, he will cease to reason; he will be a mere plaything of other people's thoughts.
>
> Instead of keeping him mewed up in a stuffy room, take him out into a meadow every day; let him run about, let him struggle and fall again and again, the oftener the better; he will learn all the sooner to pick himself up. The delights of liberty will make up for many bruises. My pupil will hurt himself oftener than yours, but he will always be merry; your pupils may receive fewer injuries but they are always thwarted, constrained and sad. I doubt whether they are any better off.
>
> (Rousseau, 1974, pp.142, 131, 42)

> To imposition from above is opposed expression and cultivation of individuality; to external discipline is opposed free activity; to learning from texts and teachers, learning through experience; to acquisition of isolated skills and tehniques by drill, is opposed acquisition of them as means of attaining ends which make direct vital appeal.
>
> (Dewey, 1963, p.19)

Perhaps the most important consideration is that experiential learning generates enthusiasm and interest in the pupils. They become directly and actively involved with the content, and (relatively) free of instruction from the teacher, which can act as a great motivator to learning. There are some current buzzwords in education to describe this process; one is that it gives 'ownership' of the lesson to the pupils, that is, the content and the resultant learning experiences become *theirs,* and their dependence on the teacher to be told what to see and learn is at least partly removed. Even if the term 'ownership' is inappropriate, there is a degree of consensus about the benefits of involving pupils in their own learning. Anyone who has been in a classroom, whether at school, college, or even at work, where the person in charge of the lesson/session has simply talked at them, will know that, unless the performance was exceptional, the most common word used afterwards is 'boring'. The lessons/sessions which get positive feedback are those which involve the learners, whether in discussions, arguments, projects, presentations or whatever. Learners of all ages expect lessons/sessions to be stimulating, interesting and wherever possible to actively encourage their participation. They will expect the teacher to seek their opinions and to be interested in them. They hope the teacher will 'allow' discussion, and teach by employing a variety of stimuli.

Most subjects taught in schools already have an experiential component within them. Art, technology and drama are based on the idea of pupils doing, making and performing things for themselves. Language and literature rely on pupils experiencing texts and using linguistic skills. PE develops skills through individual practice. Science encourages direct experience through experiment and observation. Even history has recently sought to encourage empathy as a key skill. In making pedagogical judgements, therefore, it is often helpful for student teachers to reflect on the sorts of lessons they would respond to best if they were having to 'experience' the lesson instead of teach it; that is, if they were the pupil rather than the teacher.

Pupil, Teacher and Curriculum

In reality, pedagogical judgements require the relative needs and interests of three constituents to be weighed against each other. First, there are the pupils. Each group, and each individual within a group, will respond differently to different types of teaching approaches and teacher/pupil relationships. The teacher has to become familiar with the techniques which work best with particular groups and employ them whenever possible. This is to highlight again the implications of comprehensive entitlement to education. It is the responsibility of teachers to respond and adapt to the people who are in front of them, and one of the things this involves is tailoring their pedagogy to the particular abilities and strengths of their pupils. There are those who take the view that there are no teachers of *subjects,* only teachers of *children,* the child-centred view. Such educationists and teachers argue against any separation of the academic from the pastoral elements of schooling, and highlight the needs of the child in determining the nature of what is to be taught and how it is to be taught. Supporters of such views are likely to define success in education in terms wider than mere academic success. They will highlight the importance of factors such as personal development, social skills, the ability to form relationships, and the confidence to make critical evaluations and independent judgements.

The second element which has to be considered in making pedagogical judgements is the content of the curriculum. Teachers are charged with protecting the integrity of the material which has to be taught. Some teachers highlight this aspect of their job as the most important element. They may well measure their success in terms of the enthusiasm shown by pupils for their subject, perhaps by the numbers who choose it as an option, and eventually by the number and quality of pupils who choose to study it to a higher level. Such teachers show great respect for the integrity of their subject content and specific subject skills, and work hard to ensure that their pupils grasp these and can work with them. They see their primary task as the passing on of a body of knowledge and skills to their pupils, which are to be learnt and then employed in subject examinations, both in school and, perhaps, in higher education. The introduction of a National Curriculum has specified more prescriptively than ever before the precise nature of the skills and bodies of knowledge which teachers are required (by law) to teach. This, coupled with the national testing programme, has significantly increased the necessity for subject-based teaching.

...the teacher presented material structured in accordance with convention or with such personal views on the matter as he might have. He was...concerned to transmit the accepted, and the children absorbed and if necessary regurgitated (in 'tests' or examinations) what they had acquired. The disciplines involved were subjects which had gradually been added to the curriculum and which were thought to constitute what a broadly educated man needed to know.

(Bantock, in Cox and Dyson, 1971, p.108)

An educated man must have a certain minimum of general knowledge. Even if he knows very little about science and cannot add or subtract, he must have heard of Mendel and Kepler. Even if he is tone deaf he must know something about Debussy and Verdi... But I have come across cases in which these names, or their equivalents, have been unknown to undergraduates.... It is not a question of useless or obsolete knowledge learnt by rote but of, at lowest, reference points without which it is impossible to navigate the seas of our culture.

(Conquest, in Cox and Dyson, 1971, pp.64–5)

Among [those who adopted] the most formal teaching methods... teachers... had been remarked to be conscientious, attentive to detail, impersonal and all well organised, while.... [informal teachers]... were characterised by readiness to switch attention and divert to something of immediate interest, concern for global effects rather than precise detail and dislike of tight organisational schedules. The former valued orderliness, obedience to rules, attentiveness, timetable regularity, desks arranged in rows and so on, while the latter preferred spontaneity of responding, enthusiasm, individuality of contribution, no timetable limitations and informal seating.

(Leith, in Entwistle, 1988, p.238)

If student teachers have entered teaching specifically to teach their subject, then these are the sorts of considerations which will affect their choice of teaching styles and methods. Student teachers do not necessarily have to take sides in this debate between child-centred and subject-centred approaches. However, in deciding on particular teaching methods for different content and for different groups, they will inevitably find themselves in the territory of this debate. The teacher, in making any decision on teaching and learning styles, is always in the middle between pupil and content. It is a professional skill to be able to balance concern for the pupils with concern for what they are required to learn. Student teachers have to learn how to make these judgements if they are, eventually, to become effective practitioners.

Finally, there is a third factor to consider in making pedagogical decisions, one often largely ignored by student teachers. In deciding on teaching styles and strategies and on ways of bringing pupils and content together, teachers also have to bear in mind their own particular strengths and weaknesses. Most student teachers' first experience of teaching in the classroom is with small groups of pupils, or even with individual pupils. Most, though not all, find this relatively rewarding and straightforward. Mentors are often able to comment to student teachers early in their practice that 'communication skills, one-to-one, are excellent', particularly if they have shown a genuine interest in both the pupil and their work.

But the importance of this success with teaching one-to-one or in small groups is underestimated by many student teachers who are only too ready to leave behind this method of teaching when, as they see it, they move into the 'big time' of whole-class teaching. Pedagogical judgements on teaching practice are often influenced by the idea that teachers are not teaching properly unless they are standing at the front of a classroom by a black/white board, talking, with pupils held in rapt attention, passively listening.

Very often a first lesson plan is written along the following lines:

10.00 a.m.	introduce lesson
10.05 a.m.	explain...
10.20 a.m.	demonstrate...
10.35 a.m.	conclude...
10.45 a.m.	get pupils to begin....

Such a plan implicitly places one teaching style (the teacher-led) above that of any other, as if this were the only true model of teaching. Such a lesson plan ensures that the teacher spends most of the time talking to (or at) the whole group, and that the role of the pupils will be largely passive, not asked actually to do anything until at least halfway through the lesson. Two points can be made here. First, if a student teacher has already displayed a particular strength in working with small groups, there is no need exclusively to design lessons which do not play to those strengths. Just because a student teacher is given 'a whole group' does not mean that they have to teach the whole of the group from the front of the classroom the whole of the time. Indeed, the skills required to teach successfully and appropriately from the front to a whole group are complex, and are gained slowly with experience and confidence.

Second, student teachers cannot disregard how important one-to-one contact is with pupils, and its effectiveness in producing successful learning. For many pupils it is the most effective form of help, support and motivation. Student teachers need to ensure that time for this sort of contact is planned for in their lessons. Time spent forming such relationships before taking on whole-group teaching can make the latter a great deal more effective when the time finally comes.

To summarize, there are three considerations to be balanced in making pedagogical decisions about how to bring together pupils and curriculum material. They are: the abilities and strengths of the pupils, the integrity of the subject matter, and the teacher's own particular strengths. What this means for comprehensive teachers is that they learn to mediate between pupil and content, and that this mediation, this intervention, is precisely what teaching is.

The teacher as mediator

Pedagogy has been described here not as a method or a science, but as the way teachers decide to intervene and to mediate between pupil and content in attempting to meet the obligations which comprehensive education places upon them. However, the manner of this intervention has become a highly controversial political issue, particularly for those who are not themselves teachers. The issue of teaching methods and teaching styles has been seized upon by politicians trying to argue that standards have fallen, that the basics are being ignored, that children are being allowed to decide what they want to learn instead of being told. As well as John Major's recent 'Back to Basics' campaign, this type of reaction reached its peak in the 1970s with James Callaghan's Great Debate and with the publication of the Black Papers. They were, in turn, a reaction to the Plowden Report of 1967 which had stated its own case for child-centred education, arguing that 'finding out has proved better than being told'. Equally, there are criticisms from more libertarian teachers who argue that all intervention is an oppression of the pupil and a restriction upon their natural freedom to learn, enquire and develop.

A (primary) school is not merely a teaching shop, it must transmit values and attitudes. It is a community in which children learn to live first and foremost as children and not as future adults.... The school sets out deliberately to devise the right environment for children, to allow them to be themselves and to develop in the way and at the pace appropriate to them. It tries to equalise opportunities and to compensate for handicaps. It lays special stress on individual discovery, on first hand experience and on opportunities for creative work. It insists that knowledge does not fall into neatly separate compartments and that work and play are not opposite but complementary. A child brought up in such an atmosphere at all stages of his education has some hope of becoming a balanced and mature adult and of being able to live in, and contribute to, and look critically at the society of which he forms a part. (para. 505)

Finding out has proved to be better for children than being told. (para. 1233)

44

It is not possible to describe a standard of attainment that should be reached by all or most children. (para. 551)

(The Plowden Report, DES, 1967)*

National monitoring of basic standards by examination for all children at the ages of 7,11,14 or 15 should be introduced. The school results of these tests should be available to parents, school governors and the local community. Children's names should not be published, but parents have a right to know the comparative achievements of schools.... The 14 or 15 plus examination could be used as a leaving examination, and should test basic literacy and numeracy, and a body of knowledge we should expect all our citizens to acquire. If they fail, they must return to school and sit it again at 16.... Special academic schools could be reintroduced for some 20–40% of children.... The direct grant schools should be reabsorbed into the state system and used as super-selective academic schools to keep scholarship alive and show the standards possible with bright children.

(The Black Papers, Cox and Dyson, 1977, p.8)*

I am sad to tell you that one in four of our children leave secondary education and can't read properly, can't write properly and are not competent in arithmetic.... A choking miasma of educationalist theory that despises grammar, looks down on vocabulary, derides the well-stocked mind.... Far too much well-meaning theorising nonsense is poked at our children in schools and I will not mince my words. I think that is a betrayal of our children's prospects in schools and no government could, or should stand aside from it....

I'll never forget a male teacher on a T.V. documentary, he was holding up a page of paper and it had blots and words and every fifth letter was spelt the wrong way round. That's pretty good he said; that boy is trying to tell us something. Too true he was, he was trying to tell us, poor lad, that he hadn't been well taught, that he'd been let down by the school.... He was trying to tell us his future would be less adequate than it would have been if he'd really been taught to read and write and add up and emerge from school with good qualities and good manners.

(John Major, speech 251/93, Conservative Research Department)

When issues of pedagogy are discussed in the political forum, the impression is often and easily given that didactic, subject-centred, teacher-centred instruction and experiential, child-centred learning are mutually exclusive. In addition, politicians often seem to think that the professional judgements of teachers have the least significant part to play in pedagogical decisions. Both of these impressions are incorrect. With regard to the latter, it is the case that judgements about appropriate pedagogies *have* to be made by teachers. Intervention and mediation are both inevitable and desirable if universal entitlement is to be a reality. If a teacher decides that a more child-centred approach in the classroom is right then that is a professional judgement made on the grounds that it is the most appropriate and effective method for those particular pupils, and is likely to produce the most success for them. It may be, with another class in another school that the teacher decides that a didactic, knowledge-based, information-giving session is most appropriate. Again, the decision can only be defended according to the professional judgement of the teacher that they are choosing the most appropriate method, and the one most likely to realize the entitlement of every pupil.

With regard to the former impression, that the two pedagogical methods are mutually exclusive, any polarization into two opposing camps does not reflect the realities of teaching. Student teachers need not feel that they have to be seen to be in favour of one style over another. Indeed, a teacher who accepts the obligation to offer appropriate and successful learning experiences to their pupils cannot, at the same time, stubbornly cling to one method as best in all circumstances for all pupils. Most teachers, in fulfilling their professional responsibilities, use both approaches in varying combinations.

Teachers, unlike those outside the profession, recognize that the reality of pedagogical judgements is far more complex and delicate than the rhetoric. The rhetoric forgets or does not recognize that the teacher can never represent just the pupil or the content. To become a teacher is to accept that one is always placed in the middle, and professionally obliged to combine the two in the way most likely to produce effective learning for all. This flexibility is one of the main ways that equal value can be achieved in practice. The political rhetoric surrounding pedagogy fails to grasp that the teacher is *always* the mediator between the content and the pupil. Professional decisions regarding pedagogy are always teacher-centred to begin with, even if the decision which is made is to make the lessons as experiential and child-centred as possible. Even the most progressive and libertarian educational pedagogies begin as decisions made by teachers.

Too often in the history of English education, teacher intervention has not achieved, or even aimed at achieving, an appropriate balance between the needs of the pupil and of the content. Schooling in England from the Middle Ages at least up to the turn of the 20th century was characterized by pedagogy which allowed knowledge and content to dominate the pupil. The child's own abilities and interests were disregarded in the interests of Latin, Greek and the rules of grammar. The curriculum changed little from the *Trivium* (Latin grammar, rhetoric and dialectic) and the *Quadrivium* (astronomy, geometry, music and mathematics), apart from the introduction of the study of the Scriptures. The emphasis throughout was on copying rather than creating, memorizing rather than experiencing, and on punishment rather than differentiation. It is no coincidence that when the balance was so heavily swayed in favour of content over pupil that many, often ingenious methods of forcing pupils to pay attention had to be employed. The tradition of this one-sided form of pedagogy is also the tradition of the punishment, often cruel and vicious, of the pupils who would not, or could not adapt themselves to the demands of the content.

Westminster school in the 17th century

About a quarter of an hour after five in the morning we were called up by one of the Monitors of the chamber; and after Latin prayers we went into the cloysters to wash, and thence in order, two by two, to the schoole, where we were to be by six of the clock at furthest. Between six and eight we repeated our grammar parts (Latin and Greek); fourteen or fifteen of us being selected and called out to stand in a semicircle before the Mr. and other scholars and there repeat four or five leaves in either.... After this we had two exercises that varied every other morning. The first morning we made verses *extempore* Latin and Greek authors and they of the next two forms were called to give an account of it some other part of the day; or else they were all of them to repeat and pronounce distinctly without book some of an author that had been learned the day before.

[After exercises] we had the practice of *Dictamina;* one of the fifth form being called out to translate some sentences out of an unexpected author *(extempore)* into good Latin; and then one of the sixth or seventh form to translate the same *(extempore)* into good Greek. Then the Mr. himself expounded some part of a Latin or Greek author in prose, another in verse, wherein we were to be practised in the afternoon.

At dinner and supper time are read some portion of the Latin Bible....

[Between one and three a Latin or Greek text] was to be exactly gone through by construing and other grammatical ways, examining all the Rhetorical figures, and translating it out of verse into prose, or out of prose into verse, out of Greek into Latin, or out of Latin into Greek.

Then we were enjoined to commit that to memory against the next morning.

...at other times, other faults were often punished by scholastical tasks, as repeating whole orations out of Tullie, Isocrates, Demosthenes, or speeches out of Virgil, Thucydides, Xenophon, Euripides, etc.

(Monroe, 1905, pp.525–6)

Ingenious punishments

In ancient Greece

In home discipline the sandal was used against the child's naked body, and at school we know that one method of formal punishment used was where the schoolmaster instructs two other boys to hoist the victim upon their backs so that his body will present a good target for the application of the leather strap.

(Beck, 1964, p.104)

In the Middle Ages
The tedium of long hours in school on hard benches was dispelled by liberal use of the rod. Masters faced with controlling very large classes for very long hours hardly expected to keep order by any other means, and their command of the art was as great as their itch to demonstrate it was frequent. The birch was their inseparable companion, and in sixteenth century Cambridge when the schoolmaster's degree of 'master of grammar' was conferred, the new graduate demonstrated his prowes by ceremonially flogging a shrewd boy, who received 4d for his labour.

(Orme, 1973, pp.127–8)

German schoolmaster in latin grammar school, 1750
In the course of his fifty one years and seven months as a teacher, he had, by a moderate computation, given 911,527 blows with a cane, 124,010 blows with a rod, 20,989 blows and raps with a ruler, 136,715 blows with the hand, 10,235 blows over the mouth, 7,905 boxes on the ear, 1,115,800 raps on the head, 22,763 *notabenes* with the Bible.... He had 777 times made boys kneel on peas, 613 times on a triangular piece of wood, had made 3001 wear the jackass, and 1707 hold the rod up, not to mention various more unusual punishments he had continued on the spur of the moment.

(Cubberley, 1920, pp.455–6)

18th and 19th century English elementary schools
Lancaster worked out an elaborate code of rewards and punishments, among which was 'the log', a piece of wood weighing four to six pounds, which was fixed to the neck of the child guilty of his or her first talking offence. On the least motion one way or another the log operated as a dead weight on the neck.... More serious offenders found their appropriate punishment in the Lancastrian code; the 'caravan', pillory and stocks, and 'the cage'. The latter was a sack or basket in which more serious offenders were suspended from the ceiling.

(Dickens, 1969, pp.23–4)

There have been experiments in education, from the mid-eighteenth century onwards, which have tried to push the balance firmly in the other direction, and where the interests of the child have dominated what is to be learnt, how, and when. A popular criticism of this thoroughly child-centred approach is that children are unable and unwilling to find out everything for themselves. They do not know how to select that which is required to be known, and will inevitably avoid that which may be important but difficult or dull.

Student teachers who are determined to give their pupils as much control as possible over their own learning will find several things standing in their way. First, if it is not a method of learning with which the pupils are familiar they will not, in all likelihood, understand what is being asked of them, or why. At best they may treat such lessons as a curiosity, at worst as 'a doss'. Such an experience does neither the confidence nor the reputation of the student teacher any good. Second, the very existence of a National Curriculum makes pupil control over their own learning more difficult to achieve in schools. A subject-based curriculum imposed by law inevitably has an impact on how one can teach, and one written in terms of knowledge and content inevitably sways the pedagogical balance in that direction.

Equally, however, student teachers who go into their teaching practice as 'lecturers', determined to fill the minds of their pupils with as much information and knowledge as possible, will also find out very quickly that pupils often fight back for a fairer balance between themselves and the content. If the pupils are not interested, if they will not listen, if they constantly mess around, might it not be that they are giving the student teachers an important message about their pedagogical judgements? Might it be that the pupils' restlessness is really a sign that the student teacher has not taken the pupils sufficiently into consideration in planning the lessons, and that the balance is too heavily swayed against the pupil in favour of the content?

In either of these cases, the response has to be the same. Teachers are required to reassess their judgements regarding the most appropriate and effective styles of teaching for their particular group. They have to try and realign the balance between the needs of the pupils and of the content by adjusting their teaching methods so that the balance is more appropriate to what faces them, and therefore their teaching more effective. The student teacher often believes that control in the classroom is the main criterion of a successful lesson. There are many times, however, when the answer to better relations in the classroom is not more 'discipline', but a wiser and more carefully considered method of teaching. What is most likely required is a method more in line with the demands of the comprehensive principles of unconditional entitlement and equal value, one which measures the appropriateness, effectiveness and success of a lesson by its being planned and taught to address and meet the identified learning requirements of the pupils. One of the most important skills, therefore, in turning pedagogical judgements into actual success in the classroom is *differentiation,* or teacher intervention between pupil and content to ensure that both are suitable to meet the needs and requirements of the other.

CHAPTER FOUR

Differentiation

What is differentiation?

Differentiation is a skill employed by teachers in designing, planning and presenting lessons which meet and fulfil every pupils' entitlement to education. It can be defined as:

> the means by which a teacher intervenes in every pupil's education in order to provide effective and relevant access for them to the curriculum.

The appropriateness of the curriculum itself for any particular pupil forms part of the pedagogical judgements which teachers must make in bringing the two together. Less differentiation sways the pedagogical balance in favour of the content, whilst more differentiation favours adapting the content to meet the needs of the pupils. Understood in this sense, differentiation is one of the most important ways in which a teacher's pedagogical judgements regarding the relative needs and demands of pupils and content are put into practice. As such, differentiation is also a key strategy in ensuring that the aims of universal comprehensive state education are realized for each pupil.

New teachers are required to develop the ability to differentiate. In a practical sense it needs to be evident in their lesson planning, their resources, their relationships, and in their *comprehensive* expectations. But they also need to understand how differentiation supports the entitlement of their pupils. Teachers have to differentiate in order to provide access to the curriculum for all levels of ability and, crucially, to demonstrate a commitment to value pupil success at all levels equally. These two aspects of teaching in comprehensive education are examined later in this chapter.

Like pedagogy, differentiation has a long and detailed history, one which reveals sharp differences in its function and in its implementation. Differentiation has not always been seen as a pedagogical classroom activity. It has more commonly been something which the whole *system* of education was designed to produce, and not just between pupils, but between whole social classes, to ensure their separation from each other. A *differentiated system* of educational provision is one which provides different sorts of schools for different sorts of pupils. Depending on the shade of political opinion, such a *differentiated system* is either the method by which a ruling elite maintained their own social dominance, or the method by which educational opportunities are opened up to the underprivileged. A brief exploration of this historical background helps to put current issues surrounding the theory and practice of differentiation into a clearer light for the new teacher.

Differentiation as selection

A society which selects different types of pupils for different sorts of education and schooling has a *differentiated system* of education. What might vary from one society to another are the criteria upon which selection for each type of school is based, and the purposes behind that selection. However, a differentiated system of education must inevitably involve selection.

> ...God, as he was fashioning you, put gold in those of you who are capable of ruling; hence they are deserving of most reverence. He put silver in the auxiliaries, and iron and copper in the farmers and the other crafstmen.
>
> (Plato, 1992, p.97)

In the history of European schooling, selection and inequality of access have ensured the exclusion of particular individuals or groups from certain types of education. As long ago as 400BC Plato was arguing that his ideal Republic needed to be based on a positive differentiation of the type of education which the population was to receive. He saw society as consisting of, and being organized around, three types of people. Highest on the social scale were the philosopher kings who were to enjoy one type of education. Next were the guardian auxiliaries who received a less sophisticated education, and finally the ordinary citizens who received a different schooling to either of the others. Education was an entitlement for all citizens, but the *type* of education which each was entitled to depended solely upon the role each was destined to play in society. Differentiated educational provision was the means by which each person was selected and trained for their particular station in life.

Differentiation in the system of English schooling was introduced as early as the Middle Ages with cathedral schools and remained, in various forms, up to the 1944 Education Act and, in some areas, beyond that. The grammar schools of Ancient Rome taught grammar and rhetoric to those who were destined to become the political leaders of the day. In England, this tradition was continued after the Middle Ages, through the Renaissance, the Reformation and beyond, by the endowed grammar schools and the great public schools. The teaching of Latin and Greek (grammar) ensured a clear and unambiguous differentiation between those who were to go to university and enter the professions, and those who were not. Secondary schooling became the preserve of those requiring an education befitting the gentlemen who were to go to Oxford and Cambridge, and then into law, medicine and the Church. Selection for secondary education after the Middle Ages was based almost exclusively on class and wealth, and its curriculum serviced the needs of the professions. Secondary education thus ensured a complete separation of and differentiation between the social classes.

Education for the few

Latin was the language of the Christian religion, in which its sacred texts, its liturgy, theology and law were all inserted... the mastery of the language was an essential preliminary to all higher studies.

(Orme, 1973, pp.87–8)

...grammar is the foundation, gate and source of all the other liberal arts, without which such arts cannot be known.... By the knowledge of grammar justice is cultivated and the property of the estate of humanity is increased....

(Foundation deed of Winchester College, from Leach, 1911, p.321)

God made Latin and Greek the language of many lands, that his Gospel might speedily bear fruit far and wide.... The languages are the scabbard in which the word of God is sheathed....[and] in which the jewel is enshrined.

(Luther, from Binder, 1970, p.163)

It was neccesary that the priests should understand something of that sacred and learned language in which they were to officiate; and the study of the Latin language therefore made, from the beginning, an essential part of university education.

(Smith, 1977, p.251)

When thought was finally given to the need to educate the children of the industrial working class, around the turn of the 19th century, the *type* of schooling provided for them was that deemed appropriate and necessary for such a low station in life. Church elementary schools, taking pupils from 5–14, tried to instil Christian morals, a work ethic, and a respect for authority into the next generation of workers. This dual system of education offered elementary schools for the working classes and kept secondary education, in the form of grammar schools and the public schools, reserved for the professional classes. Selection and recruitment for schooling according to social background was ensured because secondary education was not free, and social mobility was successfully prevented since secondary education was the prerequisite for entry to university and the professions. Thus, a differentiated system of education which offered one type of school to the poor, another to the rich, acted as a selection procedure for rank and privilege for the whole of English society.

Education for 'hoi polloi' ('the many')

The object in forming establishments of this nature... is to train the infant Poor to good and orderly habits – to instil into their minds an early knowledge of their civil and religious duties – to guard them, as far as possible, from the seductions of vice – and to afford them the means of becoming good Christians, as well as useful and industrious Members of Society.

(Kennington Oval Elementary school, August, 1828,
from Silver and Silver, 1974, p.1)

The lower classes ought to be educated to discharge the duties cast upon them. They should also be educated that they may appreciate and defer to a higher cultivation when they meet it; and that the higher classes ought to be educated in a very different manner, in order that they may exhibit to the lower classes the higher education to which, if it were shown to them, they would bow down and defer.

(Robert Lowe, 1867, in Sylvester, 1974, p.35)

The elementary school was preeminently an institution for the socialisation of children who were destined to be third class citizens. It originated in a society in which rigid class distinctions were regarded as God-given and unalterable.

(Richmond, 1978, pp.33–4)

The 1944 Butler Education Act made two important interventions into this situation. First, it made primary, and secondary education in particular, an entitlement for *all* children, regardless of background, wealth or influence. Second, the Act tried to replace selection in schooling according to background by selection according to ability. A place at a secondary school was no longer to be achieved by the ability to pay, but on individual merit according to a child's mental capacity as measured by the 11 plus test. Selection by ability made necessary a variety of schools which were differentiated not by cost but by curriculum, and this was institutionalized in the tripartite system: secondary grammar schools were to cater for academic children likely to enter university; secondary technical schools were designed for children with a particular talent for the sciences and arts; and secondary modern schools for those with more practical interests.

Over the next 20 years, research consistently showed that despite the attempt to introduce selection by ability and on merit, home background and social class were still major influences in determining which pupils gained places at which schools. The new tripartite system, in theory differentiating according to ability, in practice still selected mostly middle-class pupils for the grammar schools, ensuring their continued access to university and the professions.

The tripartite system, by making selection an integral part of its operation, made its aim of 'parity of esteem' between the three types of schools virtually impossible. People came to believe that, above all else, the education offered by the schools was differentiated in terms of status and opportunities. This institutionalization of differentiation came to be seen as a major obstacle to equal entitlement for all, because the system clearly did not give an equal value to each type of schooling. By the early 1960s it was being argued that offering different types of schools could only ever lead to discrimination and selection of some over others, and to a hierarchy of schools and pupils. The demand grew for the three types of schools, their three types of pupils, and the three types of educational opportunities they offered, to be replaced by one common or comprehensive school. It was hoped by its supporters that such a move would end once and for all the relationship between social class and educational achievement.

Differentiation by ability

There are diversities of gifts, and for that reason there must be diversity of educational provision. [Secondary education] should be sufficiently elastic and contain schools of sufficient variety of type, to meet the needs of all children.... Thus, all go forward, although along different paths. Selection by differentiation takes the place of selection by elimination.

(Hadow Report, 1926, from Simon, 1974, p.130)

[The Norwood Report, 1943] reognised the pupil who is interested in learning for its own sake... the pupil whose interests and abilities lie

markedly in the field of applied science or applied art... and the pupil who
deals more easily with concrete things than with ideas.

(Lawson and Silver, 1973, p.422)

The separation of the three types of school is... bound to perpetuate the
classification of children into industrial as well as social strata.... So long as
this stratification of children at eleven remains, it is in practice useless to
talk of parity of esteem in education or equality of opportunity in later life.

(TUC, 1938, from Simon, 1974, p266)

We conclude that in the field of public education the doctrine of 'separate
but equal' has no place. Separate educational facilities are inherently
unequal.

(US Supreme Court ruling, 1964, from Simon, 1991, p.273)

The introduction of comprehensive schools aimed at replacing a system
which selected according to social class or ability with one which did not
select at all. As such, pupils would not be differentiated on any grounds
other than individual educational needs, and even here, those needs were
to be met in ways which did not rank those needs or compare some more
favourably or unfavourably to others. However, in the 30 years since the
introduction of comprehensive schools, institutional differentiation has
never been entirely removed from the system. Grammar schools
continued in some areas, private education and church schools remained,
and more recently, City Technology Colleges and 'opted out', grant-
maintained schools have been created. The funding available for these
last two and the gradual introduction of (often hidden) selection criteria,
differentiates them from mainstream LEA comprehensive schools.

However, comprehensive teachers still work in schools which are *not*
selective. The system may still offer pathways through education
differentiated by resources, funding, access and influence, but
comprehensive teachers still have to be prepared for any and all children,
accepting them solely on a 'need to learn' basis. This commitment places a
particularly heavy responsibility on such teachers with regard to
differentiation, for it is now one of the most important teaching skills which
can be employed in ensuring that this comprehensive intake has a
successful education. It demands an education be provided which is
appropriate to individual needs, yet not differentiated in terms of extrinsic
value or worth. When differentiation (in theory) ceased to be institutionally
grounded in the system, the need for differentiation moved into the
comprehensive classroom and became a pedagogical and a professional
judgement, rather than merely an instrument of political power.

Differentiation as comprehensive entitlement

Differentiation poses a paradox for comprehensive teachers. Comprehensive education *per se* requires that they do not favour the education offered to one sort of pupil over another, and yet successful differentiation requires them to treat pupils differently according to their particular needs. They have to treat all pupils the same, whilst at the same time treating them all differently.

The idea of equality which lies at the heart of comprehensive education is that the education of all pupils is of equal worth and equal value. This is because, in principle, the entitlement to education of one child is equal to that of every other child. However, equality of entitlement *in principle* and *in theory* is not necessarily equality *in practice*. Simply allowing children access to free education, although treating them all the same in one sense, does not guarantee that their entitlement is realized in the classroom.

Differentiation is the key to putting a child's entitlement to education into practice. It enables teachers to intervene between pupils and content in such a way that their entitlement becomes more than just a right in principle, and is actually and successfully achieved by every pupil. An entitlement to education is something which teachers have to bring about for their pupils through their own pedagogical skills and judgements. It requires to be *produced* in the classroom by bringing pupil and content together in appropriate and relevant ways. Looked at in this way, the paradox noted above that comprehensive education requires pupils to be treated the same and differently, is perfectly encapsulated in teachers' pedagogical judgements and comprehensive commitments. Pupils are treated the same in that the entitlement of each is equally respected and valued. They are treated differently according to individual needs and requirements so that their access to, and success with, the curriculum becomes a reality.

Equality

The concept of equality in education, therefore, is in fact entirely opposite to the notion of sameness and uniformity, of turning out all children to one pattern. It is rather the concept of equal *worth,* that is, all equally deserving and needing such aids to personal growth as we can give.

(Pedley, 1969, p.23)

Unlike a selective system of education which differentiates according to criteria of ability or wealth, differentiation in the comprehensive classroom is on the basis of need. All needs are valued equally, but met in many different ways. Comprehensive teachers, unlike selective teachers, have to ensure that they do not introduce any prerequisites regarding access or entitlement which could be seen to value one child more highly than another.

If comprehensive teachers are to use differentiation to ensure success in education for all pupils, then it is important that they value the success of every pupil, whatever the level(s) the pupils are working at. If teachers work with an undifferentiated notion of success and failure in their classrooms, they will be unable to practise equal value. They will be working with only one definition of success against which every pupil's performance will be measured. Teachers, having differentiated in terms of needs, must also differentiate in their definitions of success. Success has to be judged relative to the levels of work which pupils have been set, and their responses to the work. Success in education for teacher and pupil cannot be defined by a standardized measurement applied in all cases to all situations (the problems caused by externally imposed definitions are explored later in this chapter). What counts as success is itself differentiated in the comprehensive classroom according to the pupils within it. Indeed, fixed definitions of success and failure in education have little meaning in the classroom when they are not related to the abilities of the pupils concerned. It is only with differentiated definitions of success, relative to what pupils can and cannot be expected to achieve, that success actually becomes possible for all pupils. Moreover, there are many things at which pupils will succeed which are not directly related to the formal curriculum. Definitions of success have to be wide enough to ensure that these, too, are recognized and valued.

However, teachers also recognize that no success at whatever level or work is ever complete. Differentiation designed to meet the learning needs of pupils has always to recognize that one of those needs is to move on and to develop. Successful differentiation, in responding to some needs, will create new ones which are to be addressed in future lessons. This is necessary to ensure progression and development.

Recognizing the need for *success at every level* is a key component to understanding the importance of differentiation in comprehensive education. To value success at every level is part of ensuring that the rhetoric of equality of entitlement becomes a reality. Even though the work of some pupils will be of a higher or lower (normative) standard compared to others, nevertheless successful and effective differentiation will pass on to pupils that their particular success is valued as much as anyone else's by their teacher. Whatever level a pupil has achieved, and will achieve, it is an achievement *for them*, and stands apart from normative comparisons as an achievement.

In summary, differentiation in comprehensive education has two basic elements. First, that lessons are planned and work is set which is sufficiently comprehensive and wide ranging (i.e., differentiated) both to meet the existing needs of all pupils and to anticipate and create new ones in order to ensure progression and development. Second, that having differentiated the work, teachers respect and value equally the levels of success which their pupils achieve. Comprehensive coverage and equal value are the two professional and pedagogical requirements for successful differentiation in the comprehensive classroom. They are what new teachers are required to learn and to become skilled in, if their own practice is to be relevant, effective and successful for their pupils.

Achieving differentiation

It has been common for teachers to adopt one of two methods to achieve differentiation: by task and by outcome.

Differentiation by task

To ensure that the work given to a pupil or to groups of pupils is appropriate to their particular ability level(s), different schemes of work need to be written by the teacher for different sorts of pupils. To give all pupils the same work, or the same assignments, is to ignore the fact that some will be able to complete them easily whilst others will find them very difficult. Differentiation requires that teachers should really be ensuring that work is challenging for *all* pupils, and therefore teachers cannot sensibly give the same task to the most *and* the least able pupils. Differentiation by task, then, is where different schemes of work and different assignments are planned for by teachers to ensure that different groups of pupils are given things to do which are commensurate with their particular levels of ability.

An argument used against this approach is that differentiation by task requires a pupil's performance to be predicted, some would say labelled, before the lesson, and that those given the most simple tasks are actually prevented from achieving the full range of marks available to other pupils. Looked at in this way, differentiation by task is only another form of selection on the grounds of perceived ability. It offers different educational opportunities and experiences to different sorts of pupils by creating a differentiated curriculum within a single school. It simply reproduces the function of differentiation as a way of separating pupils from one another, and lends itself to setting and streaming. This approach does not therefore embody the requirement that comprehensive education treats pupils differently *and* the same. It lends itself to a hierarchy of courses and of groups rather than equal value, and tips the balance in favour of difference over equality. As such, differentiation by *task* is often seen as a prior differentiation of, and a labelling of, *pupils* rather than of their work.

Differentiation by outcome

In this method of differentiation, pupils are not judged on their perceived abilities or given different schemes of work to do. Instead, all pupils have access to the same schemes of work, the same activities and the same assignments, and are differentiated only according to the quality of the work they produce. Such an approach, it is argued, avoids labelling pupils or selecting one from another on the grounds of perceived ability. It gives each pupil an equal opportunity to achieve the full range of marks available, which differentiation by task does not. Also, differentiation by outcome does not require streaming or setting, as no selection of pupils is required beforehand. Pupils are therefore not judged pre-emptively according to who they are or what they have produced before, but only on the work which is produced on the course.

However, a counter to this approach is that it is simply unrealistic and often unfair to give every pupil the same work, not only because it cannot be appropriate to all of them, but because it cannot ensure that all pupils will enjoy *some* level of success. Surely it is better, the argument goes, to give pupils work at which they are going to succeed, rather than a single task at which inevitably some are going to succeed all too easily and others not at all. In trying to fulfil the requirement to treat pupils the same and different, differentiation by outcome swings the scales too much in favour of an abstract equality at the cost of responding effectively to individual needs.

Differentiation as support

When debates on differentiation remain locked in these two methodologies, and simply oppose one against the other, the broader professional responses to the issue are obscured. It is the case that most teachers in their actual practice produce a much more sophisticated approach to differentiation than either of these two methods suggest. New teachers would do well not to view differentiation as a choice between these two methods, but rather as a fundamental part of the pedagogical judgements which they are required to make in *all* their dealings with their pupils. The comprehensive requirement to treat pupils equally yet differently is not met by either of the above methods. Its competing demands find expression in the ways in which teachers *support* the learning of all their pupils. Differentiation involves professional and pedagogical judgements which ensure equal value, respond to individual needs, and aim at success for all pupils. It is through the skill of teachers in producing differentiated support for pupils that equal entitlement to success is realized.

Differentiation is best seen not as different tasks or outcomes, but as different *levels and methods of support* geared to producing a variety of levels of successful learning. This allows teachers to focus on differentiation as a pedagogical skill and as something basic in the relationship between pupil, teacher and content, rather than as a merely technical operation in presenting work. Differentiation, seen as *support* of pupil learning by the teacher who is aiming to produce success at every level, can then be seen to be integral to a variety of teaching skills, ranging from the way courses are planned and assessed, to the way a teacher talks to a pupil.

In everyday teacher/pupil contact

Teachers employ their skills of differentiation every time they have contact with or simply talk to a pupil. At various levels and in many different ways they modify that contact to suit the pupil concerned. They will try to ensure that *what* they say, and *how* they say it are appropriate and relevant to that particular pupil, and that the communication is a successful one. In particular, teachers are required to ensure that their use of language is appropriate for the person they are talking to. It is often a failing of new teachers that their language is not pitched at the right levels for their pupils. As a result their lessons, their explanations, their instructions, and most embarrassingly their jokes either go totally over the heads of their pupils, or patronize them.

Teachers differentiate when they select language which is appropriate either to a class, a small group, or most particularly to individual pupils. In seeking to ensure that their pupils understand them, teachers put into practice their equal value for each pupil. Undifferentiated communication holds the *pupil* responsible for not understanding the teacher, instead of teachers accepting their own responsibility and obligation to differentiate in their use of language so that understanding is achieved by all pupils.

Such differentiation is a necessary component of good teacher/pupil relationships where the pupil knows and can see that the teacher is interested in them as an individual. To treat a pupil as an individual, to be able to relate to them, and to form good working relationships with them, requires differentiation by the teacher. Yet the importance of differentiation in such relationships is often masked, precisely because of its everyday and taken-for-granted nature. It is seldom recognized as being a most important pedagogical skill, one which helps to fulfil the responsibilities demanded of teachers in comprehensive schools to value and make real the entitlement of every child.

In course planning

To achieve differentiation as support when planning and preparing courses and lessons, teachers are required to have an idea of the appropriate levels which need to be set for particular groups and individuals. It is often the case that student teachers are asked to prepare work for a class before they have worked with that class. Mentors need to understand the difficulties this poses for any teacher, let alone a student teacher. If this has to be the case, then consultation between student and mentor about the how, when, what and why of lessons and courses can help to prevent a great deal of anxiety and wasted time and effort.

To support pupil learning in planning courses and lessons it is important that the teacher try to predict the sorts of problems which pupils are likely to have with the content, and to plan with that in mind. It is this skill of anticipating pupil needs before they occur which enables a quick, effective and planned response to those needs when they do occur.

Any course, if it is to ensure a pupil's entitlement to the curriculum, has to make success possible for all pupils. This means planning in such a way that success is possible both throughout the course and at its completion. To avoid the labelling implicit in differentiation by task, the schemes of work can be common to all pupils. Equally, however, a course can have many ways in which pupils can succeed, both in particular lessons and at the end of a course. This avoids the tendency in differentiation by outcome to set *one* activity, task or performance by which success and failure are judged. A carefully differentiated course is planned so that success is possible at each step of the course, and that each step is acknowledged as success. The teacher is required to record beforehand the various things asked of a pupil on the course, and to plan for the different levels at which they can be achieved. This involves dividing up the schemes of work into the different skills, knowledge, concepts, etc. which together make up the whole of the course, and ensuring that success in each of these is planned for and made possible.

A mentor might expect a student teacher to try to produce course outlines which do more than simply explain what is to be taught. A complete course outline includes the overall aims of the course (the *why*), the specific objectives of each lesson and their contribution to the whole, explanations about *what* is to be taught, *when,* and most importantly, *how.* There should also be clear indications about how pupils can achieve success on the course in different ways and at different levels. It must be clear that the course is differentiated in its expectations of pupils by anticipating and planning for problems and specific needs, but it does not have to set separate schemes of work (differentiation by task), nor condemn all pupils to one exclusive route to success (differentiation by outcome).

A differentiated course rides the ambiguity between treating pupils the same and differently. It allows access to the common curriculum, yet provides for different forms of support for different pupils, and offers opportunities for success at all levels. This, in turn, requires differentiation by resources, and in marking and assessment.

In providing resources

Student teachers' first actual planning for differentiation is often in the preparation of resources. They are expected to be able to produce a variety of resources which aim to meet a variety of needs in the classroom. A common method is to produce common resources for all, and extra resources for the most and least able pupils. This approach tries to ensure that the most able are stretched beyond the demands of the common resources, and that the least able are given help which will make the common resources accessible for them. However, this provision of extra resources can itself be seen as unjustified extra work or unjustified embarrassment *unless* the resourses are specifically related to the different levels of success which have already been written into the course.

Very often it is those courses or lessons which do not incorporate equal value for different levels of success which actually build into the course or lesson an *inevitable* level of failure. A brief example may make the point.

People often remember their own PE lessons at school as a miserable, sometimes tortuous affair which seemed designed to ensure maximum humiliation, and to make people do what they could not do and did not want to do. Such lessons serve as an example in education of the success of the few at the expense of the many. To make the whole year group compete in a 100m sprint race in order that the fastest three pupils can be selected to run in the county trials is differentiation by outcome of the most severe kind. It is deliberately to design a lesson where all but three pupils can, given the stated and planned outcome, only fail.

A similar situation is created when the stated objective of a lesson is, for example, to 'play tennis'. Anyone who has ever watched pupils playing tennis at school will have noticed that often there is not a decent game to be seen, where rallies consist of one shot, and the ball disappears to all corners of the court and beyond. Pupils are failing because there is no differentiation in such a lesson. In order to fulfil the overall aim of the lesson 'play tennis', all pupils have been given the same equipment, put in the same situation, and asked to do the same thing. No thought has been given to the needs of each pupil, nor to the ways that they might be successful at playing tennis instead of failing. Why, for example, give everyone the same equipment – a full-size racket and a proper tennis ball – which accomplished players use? A differentiated lesson subdivides the overall task (play tennis) into manageable sections to provide success in the same skills but at more appropriate levels. A variety of resources, for example, half-size rackets, soft balls, playing on half the court, make success easier to achieve. It is *still* success at 'playing tennis', providing that the teacher combines this differentiation of resources with an attitude of equal value for all of the levels of success which can be achieved. And success at *any* level rather than outright failure provides the motivation to move on to other, higher levels.

The competitive ethos

A report from the Welsh Sports Council shows that around half of pupils prefer games to P.E. But a common complaint in both is the way some teachers favoured the most able pupils, leaving the rest ignored.

(*TES*, 1994b)

The Sports Minister acknowledged that not everyone enjoyed team games and competitive sport, or learned lessons from them. But [he said] neither of those undoubted truths invalidates, or contradicts, the greater truth that most children do learn deeply important lessons. This is just as important for those who are good at games as it is for those who are not.

(*TES*, 1994c)

Our job is to turn pupils on to exercise and sport, make it enjoyable, and keep them fit; does it really matter if it's football, hockey or step aerobics?
(P. Faulkner, Head of Dept., Mountbatten Secondary School, Romsey, *TES*, 1994d)

Providing a range of resources to enable success at different levels is differentiation as support of pupil learning. It allows all pupils to begin with what they can do, not with what teachers hope they can do. But, equally important, differentiation as support does not just give pupils resources appropriate to their existing needs: it builds in an enthusiasm, generated by success, to attempt new levels with other resources. Differentiated resources do not prevent success at new levels, they encourage it.

The terms differentiation by task and outcome do not adequately describe this approach to the planning of lessons or resources. Both include within them the need for pupil failure, either before the lesson has even begun, or at the end. If the real objective of the tennis lesson is to produce one tennis professional from the school, then the lesson does not have a comprehensive outlook. A comprehensive tennis lesson supports all pupils by providing the appropriate resources for their success. The goal of differentiation by support is primarily to ensure an effective and successful learning experience for all pupils, a goal which cannot be achieved if all performances are measured against an undifferentiated notion of what it is to be able to 'play tennis'.

Assessment

The relationship between assessment and differentiation as support is a difficult one. In assessing work, teachers are inevitably measuring it against one of three possible criteria. They might be comparing the work of one pupil against that of all the others and placing them in rank order; this is called norm-referencing. They might be comparing the work against a mark scheme consisting of things which have to be done to gain marks, and including a breakdown of marks available for different levels of performance; this is called criterion-referencing.

They might also be comparing the work of one particular pupil against other work produced by the same pupil and trying to decide whether the work shows improvement, development and progress. Here the criterion for comparison is the individual pupil and his or her past performance. This method is very useful for class-based diagnostic assessment, because it enables the teacher to isolate particular problems which a pupil is having and to offer a diagnosis for them. Summative assessment, often a form of end-of-term or end-of-year report, most likely includes overall comments on the individual progress and achievements of pupils.

It is unlikely that student teachers will be involved in summative assessment but, depending on the length of teaching practice, they may be involved in writing mark schemes and marking work. Differentiation as support is a very important part of this process. In setting assignments teachers have a professional responsibility to ensure that a full range of marks and learning outcomes are available. An assignment fails the pupils if it does not ask for and reward work which reflects a comprehensive range of abilities. This can be very difficult for experienced teachers to get right, never mind student teachers. Concentrating too much on the top end of the ability spectrum can lead to an assignment being set where the expectations are too high even for the majority of pupils. Similarly, concentrating too greatly on the lower end can mean that the most able are not given sufficient chance to fully stretch themselves. Often, the results which are achieved in an assignment reflect more about the way it was planned and what it asked pupils to do, than the real abilities of the pupils themselves. Teachers have to try and ensure that assignments are clear, coherent, logically progressive and *possible*. A successful assignment is one that hits the right level by, at one and the same time, hitting all the necessary levels in an appropriate and effective way.

Just as assignments have to be set to ensure differentiation and success at all levels, so, too, do mark schemes. However, differentiation in mark schemes can be used in the traditional sense as an instrument for securing selection and a hierarchy of value and worth in education. A mark scheme is inevitably a rank order of performance where some will be seen to succeed at higher levels than others. Pupils themselves in such circumstances are often very keen to know who got what and where they came in the class. Rank orders undermine equal value because they are a public acknowledgement that success at one level is below or of less value than success at another level.

Equal value of equal work

...a school which is endeavouring to operate the equal value principle will assign equal importance and give equal care and attention to the assessment of all the children's work.

(Daunt, 1975, p.60)

It is very important that our comprehensive schools shall not content themselves with merely achieving equal opportunity for the competitive success of individual pupils.... They will be shown and offered all the scholastic kingdoms, including Oxford and Cambridge, York and Canterbury. Tempting though such prizes are, they must not be allowed to divert the new schools from their larger purpose.

(Pedley, 1969, pp.205–6)

However, it is possible to make the mark scheme work as a support for pupils and it can, if designed carefully, still embody the philosophy of equal value. First, in writing a mark scheme it is important to ensure clarity in exactly what it is that marks are to be awarded for. If all pupils are to have equal access to success in the assignment, then it must be very clear what is required if success is to be achieved.

Second, a carefully differentiated mark scheme will have different levels of success built into it. It will divide itself into specific skills, concepts and outcomes, showing how rewards are available for each, and how each part then contributes to the overall mark for the final outcome(s). A supportive yet differentiated mark scheme is one which breaks the assignment up into different skills and knowledge, and into different levels of performance in those skills and that knowledge. A pupil's work can then be assessed against those levels, and a variety of marks achieved.

What is important is that the mark scheme be used to reward pupils for what they have done, rather than act as something which penalizes them for what they have not done. In terms of assessment, success and failure are defined by the mark scheme. It is the teacher's responsibility to ensure that the mark scheme rewards what the assignment as a whole enabled the pupils to show they could do. Therefore, a mark scheme and an assignment should be written together, and it should be clear from both exactly what is to be done, the various stages and levels of performance at which this can be achieved, and how marks are available for all levels. The worst practice in this area is when pupils are penalized for not doing things they were not asked to do, or are not rewarded for things they were asked to do and did.

Third, mark schemes can be used to support pupil learning and achievement if they are given to the pupils in advance and used in a way which can be easily understood. The way work is marked is often a mystery to pupils. Perhaps teachers have wanted to keep it that way, either to mask the deficiencies of their mark schemes (or their lack of mark schemes altogether), or in some way to prevent pupils from having any grounds for questioning, or even understanding, the marks they are given. New teachers can employ the strategy of giving (simplified) mark schemes to their pupils at the same time as setting the assignments, explaining to the pupils exactly what marks will be awarded for, and how they can go about achieving those marks. This has many aspects of good practice. It forces teachers to write mark schemes and assignments together, constructed around what pupils are being asked to do. It shows to the pupils in concrete terms that they will be rewarded for the work they do, and that marks are possible at all levels. It enables pupils to see that they *can* gain marks for their work, rather than just believe that they will 'not be very good'. It might sound a somewhat pedantic difference, but it can make a very great difference to pupil self-confidence and motivation.

Equally important in terms of equal value, giving out mark schemes in advance enables teachers to go through work with pupils after it has been marked and to show them, via the mark scheme, how they missed out on certain marks and what they need to do next time to improve. It is also another concrete way of judging and criticizing the work, without transferring those judgements and criticisms into labels about an individual.

Fourth, there is the professional issue about how to inform pupils of their marks. There are two concerns here, both related to returning marked pieces of work to pupils. Some methods of returning work are more in line with the professional responsibility for equal value than others. Even though the marks themselves represent a rank order, nevertheless comprehensive teachers must try to ensure that in returning the marks they are not seen to give unequal value to some levels over others. They will most likely not be helped in this by their own pupils, who seek norm-referencing in order to establish a pecking order within the group. Teachers can play down the importance of this, but probably will be unable to stop it completely. However, teachers do not need to display the marks publicly, nor call out the marks as the work is returned. They can return work personally and in relative privacy, allowing pupils to pass on their marks to others at their own discretion.

Equal value can be promoted if raw scores are coupled with teacher comments both about the relation of marks to the mark scheme, and a value-added comment relative to the pupils' own levels of achievement. In the former case, it can be good practice to show a pupil, through the mark scheme, where they gained and lost marks, so that their achievements are noted, and the necessary improvements put into a concrete form. Raw scores may give a misleading impression of achievement and success. A mark or grade may, in comparison with others, look very good or very bad, but for that particular pupil may represent an immense improvement or deterioration in their levels of achievement. It is only through a teacher's comments, additional to the raw score, that achievements are related to the individual circumstances of each pupil. It is very time-consuming for teachers, but brief personal comments, written or oral, can have the most positive effect on motivation, and can embody equal value and success at every level in a way in which raw scores cannot. New teachers will find that this kind of interest in and concern for their pupils is repaid many times over.

To sum up, differentiation as support is not the same as differentiation by task or outcome. Differentiation by support, in teacher/pupil relationships, in course planning and lesson preparation, in providing resources, in setting and marking assignments, and in returning work to pupils, puts into practice the apparently contradictory demand of comprehensive education that it treat pupils the same and differently. It does this because it embodies the desire and the commitment to value the entitlement to education of all pupils equally, and to provide each individual with the opportunities for success at whatever levels are appropriate for the realization of that entitlement.

It is worth noting that differentiation presents teachers, and therefore student teachers, with one of the most difficult challenges in comprehensive education. Student teachers will never be judged on their ability to differentiate in all the ways mentioned in this chapter. Equally, the problems which differentiation poses will vary from one curriculum subject to another. Nevertheless, it is important at the start of a career in teaching at least to be made aware of the importance of differentiation, and of its necessity in all aspects of classroom practice.

CHAPTER FIVE

Tutoring

What is a tutor?

In many schools, the academic and the pastoral are kept strictly separate. When this is the case, it is often pastoral responsibilities which are given least status. New teachers can be forgiven for hardly realizing that the role of the tutor is at all important, or even for not realizing that they will be expected to be a tutor. Teacher training courses often pay little attention to the professional responsibilities and demands of tutoring, and on teaching practice the experience can all too easily be reduced to taking a register twice a day. However, there are several important factors which make tutoring one of a teacher's primary responsibilities, and which demand that new teachers be more adequately prepared for the role.

First, the very nature of comprehensive education, with its unselected intake, means that a comprehensive school not only has a wide variety of ability amongst its pupils, but a wide variety of social and home backgrounds. Society and its 'problems' are not left outside the school gates, they are brought in with the pupils as part of their lives. Schools which acknowledge this are already likely to give greater importance to the pastoral system and the role of the tutor than are schools which do not.

Second, the National Curriculum demands that secondary schools now give curriculum time to PSHE – personal, social and health education. This work concentrates on a range of issues, from sex education to drugs and alcohol, from bullying and forms of prejudice and discrimination to forming and maintaining personal relationships, and from coping with stress, time management, etc., to preparations for further and higher education, employment or unemployment. It is common practice, although by no means universal, for tutors to have to accept responsibility for teaching PSHE to their tutor groups. There is a need, therefore, for training and preparation as early as possible in this area for new teachers.

Third, as social institutions have grown ever larger, there has developed an increasing awareness by people that they are merely tiny cogs in a giant wheel. Their own part in the process is often so small and insignificant as to be almost invisible, unacknowledged and seldom recognized as valuable. A comprehensive school which gives equal value to the entitlement of all pupils has an obligation to ensure that their pupils feel that they are valued and that none of them is allowed to slip through the net into anonymity or despair. One way of ensuring that pupils have someone in the school who is interested in them, unconditionally and without regard to the abilities they may or may not have, is to make the tutor an important source of support for a particular group of pupils.

Fourth, in their time at school, pupils often need someone to intervene on their behalf when specific needs arise. If a pastoral system is in place and works well, then the tutor is most often the person called upon to do this. It is expected that tutors know their tutees well, and in ways which are not exclusively related to their schoolwork. Therefore the tutors' perspective should provide support for pupils over and above that provided for academic work. Interventions may be required to sort out problems with other pupils, other teachers, parents, police or social services, or to provide support with applications, employment and leisure activities. Sometimes the most important thing a tutor can do is help to sort out problems with late work, devise study plans, and simply help pupils plan their time.

Finally, and most importantly, the nature of comprehensive education does not lend itself to a strict separation of the academic and the pastoral. In a system of universal and equal entitlement, the making of pedagogical judgements is both academic *and* pastoral. On the one hand, the classroom teacher, in ensuring entitlement and equal value, is also a tutor. At the very basis of comprehensive education is a care and a concern that every pupil be given the resources which will enable their personal, social, spiritual, moral, physical and academic development. Universal and free state education is an academic *and* a pastoral entitlement for all pupils. More practically, in making pedagogical judgements classroom teachers are obliged to balance the needs of curriculum material with the needs of pupils. In deciding on the former, teachers act academically; in deciding on the latter teachers act pastorally, and in bring the two together, teachers act pedagogically and professionally. Pedagogical judgements *per se* are not academic or pastoral, but rather their unification.

> ### The pastoral
>
> ...there can be no pastoral/academic split; there is rarely any curricula reality unless there is reciprocity between teacher and learner; and where there is reciprocity – wherever there is human relationship – then there is 'pastoral' work....
>
> (Marland, 1974, p.4)
>
> Personal and social development and responsibility are intrinsic to the nature of education. It is something from which no teacher can opt out.
>
> (HMI, 1989, p.1)

On the other hand, the tutors' role is also pedagogical for it too requires tutors to make judgements, to intervene, and to mediate between the pupils and various other groups of people. Tutors are required to make pedagogical judgements about the best way to bring the two sides together, again balancing the needs and requirements of each, to ensure that their meeting is effective and successful. Just as for the classroom teacher, definitions of success in any tutor mediation are dependent upon the needs of the people involved, and the demands of the situation.

New teachers *will* be tutors. They are required not only to understand the importance of the role, but to become effective and successful tutors for their pupils. However, the gap between what is expected in this regard on teaching practice, and what is expected of an NQT can be alarming. The following sections give an introduction to tutoring for new teachers, both for their time as students and as full-time newly qualified members of staff.

The student as tutor

Depending upon the length of their teaching practice, student teachers receive a variety of experiences in tutoring. Some may be asked to teach PSHE lessons, some will be given a tutor group of their own, some may only sit and observe a tutor with a group. The most common experience available to all student teachers is to be given responsibility for taking the register. Exactly what this involves will vary from school to school, and from group to group, depending on the time available and what the pupils are used to. However, neither student teachers nor their mentors can take the responsibility lightly. Being asked to 'go and take the register' may sound innocuous enough. But for student teachers, well prepared in every other aspect of their teaching practice, this situation can prove to be the one they fear the most, have least confidence and control in, and find the most difficult to manage effectively. This is aside from the added pressure that the register is a legal document from which a great deal of important information is collected and which can, in certain circumstances, be used in court as evidence.

There are two immediate pedagogical problems.The first problem is that student teachers might not know their tutor group, or even teach them. It is certainly helpful if they can be given a tutor group which they do teach, as the tutor relationship and the teacher relationship can be used to complement each other. Being given a group which is unfamiliar to them puts student teachers immediately at (at least) three disadvantages. First, they are required to register names yet they do not know any names. The scope for being messed around with in this respect is therefore very wide. Second, the original tutor and their group will hopefully have established their own effective relationship, and student teachers can be seen by the pupils as not having the 'right' to be their tutor. Pupil resentment at the 'impostor' is greater the closer their relationship is with the original tutor. Third, student teachers are unlikely to have either the time or the opportunities to experience the realities of tutoring, except for taking the register, because for serious tutoring matters pupils will have to deal with their real tutor.

The second pedagogical problem is what to do in the tutor time available. Some schools allow only five to ten minutes for tutor groups to meet, in which case there is little that can be done other than to take the register, read out notices, collect monies, etc. In schools which have longer, up to 25 minutes or more for all or some of the tutor periods, then there is the time, and most likely the expectation, that something else will be done. Student teachers put in this situation are often no longer working with material they have produced themselves, nor are they working in their own particular subject specialism. There is, therefore, great scope for student teachers to feel very vulnerable, working with an unfamiliar group and with unfamiliar material. These are all reasons why tutor time should not be taken lightly by student or mentor. In all other lessons student teachers are being asked to use their knowledge of their pupils and of their subject material to judge how best to bring the two together. In tutor time very often students have an understanding of neither, yet are still asked to teach. Without support and guidance, what is asked of student teachers in this situation borders on the unprofessional, as it makes such pedagogical judgements, and therefore pupil entitlement, very difficult to achieve successfully.

> ### *Lack of training*
>
> ...having had virtually no academic introduction to pastoral care, the concept of 'being a Tutor' is built up from snatches of advice, administrative instructions, and fleeting briefings from keen teachers on the job in such a way that tutoring is seen as a mass of detailed tasks, lacking coherence or point beyond the immediate administration.
>
> (Marland, 1989, p.3)

If student teachers are to be able to treat tutor time in the same professional way that they are expected to prepare for their lessons, then mentors need to ensure that preparation for it is thorough. Part of that preparation will be that the students know and have some relationship with the pupils, either because they teach them, or because they have spent time with them in previous tutor periods. All of the techniques used to establish a relationship with a group described in Chapter 2 are relevant here. Student teachers need to be given time to become acquainted with the various tutoring activities required of them, and to be given help and advice on the various ways in which these activities might be carried out most successfully. They need also to ensure that differentiation is not overlooked, and that every pupil's entitlement in these activities is achieved.

Planning, preparation, relationships and differentiation are all as important in tutor time as they are in other lessons. Tutor time places the same pedagogical requirements upon teachers as do subject lessons. To treat them in such a professional way is the best possible preparation student teachers can receive for the tutoring they will be called upon to do as newly qualified teachers. Student teachers will never get the full range of tutoring experiences on teaching practice because they cannot be given the full responsibilities of a tutor. They can, however, be shown that tutoring is as important as classroom teaching, requiring the same levels of professional and pedagogical judgements, sharing the same comprehensive aims of pupil entitlement and equal value, but involving infinitely more personal and often difficult situations and decisions.

The role of the tutor

In terms of pupil entitlement, the role of the tutor in a secondary school is far more comprehensive than the role of the classroom teacher. It embodies the pupils' entitlement to support with work, with friends, with teachers, with family, with relationships, with employment and unemployment, with social issues, and with personal issues and problems. Above all, the role embodies the pupils' unconditional entitlement to know that their educational needs and successes are valued by those within the institution. The tutor is most often the person who represents the school to parents, who represents a pupil to other teachers, who sometimes represents other teachers to the pupil, and who represents the interests of the pupil to whoever is required. Finally, in addition to support and representation, the tutor becomes a figure of stability in a pupil's life through all the stresses and demands which school and the curriculum place upon them. These tutoring responsibilities – *support, representation* and *stability* – are rarely, if ever, explained to student teachers, and NQTs are often wholly unprepared for the range or the importance of the tutor's role in a school. They are required to learn on the job, and to learn very quickly.

All three aspects of the role depend almost entirely upon the quality of the relationship which tutors can establish within their groups. To be able to support a pupil, tutors have to value that pupil and to have found a reason or reasons to want to support them. With a few pupils this proves very difficult, but it is still the tutors' professional responsibility to find something to value in all their tutees. It is very often the case that tutors have to forgive 'failings' in character, behaviour or motivation when other relationships (in school or outside) are breaking down for a particular pupil. Pupils who are in all sorts of trouble elsewhere still need someone, most often the tutor, to want to support them and represent them in the face of these problems.

The longer a tutor is able to be with one group, the greater are the chances that quality relationships will be established. Stability in the tutor/tutee relationship can be institutionalized by ensuring that, wherever possible, a tutor stays with one group from the time the group enters the school to the time they leave. Organizing tutor activities, visits, etc., helps to cement relationships. Equally, supporting pupils who are involved in sports teams, drama productions, charity events, etc., are all excellent ways of showing them that their abilities and contributions, in whatever field(s), are valued. Tutors are required, more than anyone else in the school, to build up an overall picture of the pupil. They are the likely to be the people who write summative reports, who talk to parents, and eventually who write references for jobs and/or further/higher education.

The tutors' relationship with pupils also has other functions. As the people who first see their pupils in the morning they are likely to be able to notice sudden changes in mood or outlook, where a pupil is unusually quiet, unhappy, disruptive, angry, etc. When such things are picked up

74

early and quickly by tutors, this can prevent further problems arising during the day. In more serious cases, a tutor may be the first person in school to notice bruising or cuts which suggest some form of abuse, or regular absences on particular days suggesting that someone or something is being avoided.

Child Abuse Procedures

All schools must have a designated teacher who deals with all child protection issues and makes contact with their police and social services counterparts. They should receive adequate training to undertake this role. They should also be provided with the names of all children in their school on the At Risk register, and all those who have contact with children on the At Risk register should be kept informed of their progress.

Continuous monitoring of children who are designated 'at risk' should take place.

All teachers should be trained to identify signs of abuse in children. Any concerns must be reported to the designated teacher or the head. A note of the teacher's concerns should also be logged.

(Child Abuse Procedures, from *TES*, 1994e)

Depending upon the organization of a school, tutors may be asked to work with certain pupils in trying to sort out behaviour problems, personality clashes, bullying, underachievement, etc. Systems may be in place which try to involve tutors if 'problems' arise with any of their tutees. This is not to suggest that teachers should simply pass on problems in their classrooms to tutors. However, those problems may be that much easier to sort out if tutors' relationships with pupils can be used to good advantage. It has the added importance of showing pupils that teachers are prepared to talk to each other and to work together in the interests of pupils, something which, after initial suspicion, can be a concrete example to pupils of their being valued.

Overall, tutors are the linchpin and the focus of pupils' whole school experience. It is the tutor, charged with supporting and representing when necessary, and offering stability to pupils, who is likely to build up the most informed picture of their overall capabilities, strengths, weaknesses and qualities. Above all, the tutor/pupil relationship has to be based on equal value, and has to measure success and worth according to the standards which are appropriate and relevant for each individual pupil. Tutors are not asked to *like* all their tutees equally. They are expected to form professional, caring relationships which are in the best interests of all their tutees, and to *value* their tutees equally, both for what they can and cannot do. The demands of tutoring can be intensely personal, and can stretch all teachers, but especially NQTs, in ways which they never expected when they thought of becoming teachers. It is the job of tutors to get involved in pupils' lives, but it is not their job to become *too* involved. To draw this line successfully, and to know when intervention is required, how much, and of what sort, is always an extremely difficult pedagogical judgement. The more fully tutors know their tutees, as well as their home backgrounds and (where relevant) their parents, the more able are tutors to intervene in ways which balance pupils' needs against the demands of whatever situation faces them. Just as a classroom teacher mediates and is in the middle between pupil and content, so a tutor is in the middle and mediates between pupil and anything (and everything) else.

Personal, Social and Health Education (PSHE)

PSHE is not a compulsory subject within the National Curriculum. Rather, it is a theme which schools are obliged to cover in some way in their curriculum. There are various ways in which this can be done. A common strategy is to set aside a period of time, perhaps a tutor period, where a PSHE course can be taught, usually by tutors to their tutor groups. Other schools have a team of teachers for whom PSHE is their main curriculum area and responsibility; this arrangement may mean that new teachers are not involved in teaching PSHE. Finally, some schools choose to teach PSHE through cross-curricula themes, ensuring that through their existing curriculum the content and issues of PSHE are raised and discussed within certain subjects and on specific courses. Schools adopting this method should be able to identify clearly where and when pupils will meet PSHE; this exercise is called 'curriculum mapping'.

As seen above, teaching requires judgements to be made about the most effective ways to bring together the curriculum and the pupil. Such judgements are always aiming to strike the appropriate balance between the needs of each, in order to produce the greatest levels of motivation and success. Whereas in the National Curriculum it is the content of academic subjects which defines curriculum areas on the timetable, with PSHE it is the personal and social lives of pupils which define timetable space. Moreover, just as the academic is always pastoral in its pedagogical judgements, so with PSHE, the pastoral becomes pedagogical in decisions made about the levels of knowledge, type of content etc., which best meets the personal and social needs of the pupils.

There need be no artificial separation between National Curriculum subjects as requiring one type of teaching and PSHE as another. Both require the same professional and pedagogical judgements, and both contribute to the obligation that schools fulfil a pupil's comprehensive entitlement.

For various reasons, PSHE suffers from a lack of status in the eyes of many teachers, parents and pupils. Nevertheless, PSHE is as deserving of the need for planning, preparation, pedagogical judgements, differentiation and equal value relationships as are all other aspects of comprehensive education. The nature of the material which has to be covered in PSHE makes for particular problems, not only professionally and pedagogically, but also morally. Each of these will now be briefly examined.

The extra professional issue raised by PSHE is not whether the area should be considered an equal part of the whole curriculum, but rather *who* in a school ought to be given the responsibility for teaching it. Student teachers are given little if any preparation or training on their courses in either the content or the methods which they might need or encounter if they are to teach PSHE. Very often it involves them teaching content far removed from their own areas of subject expertise, and sometimes teaching content which they have never come across before. It is a great danger for new teachers if PSHE material is simply treated as 'common sense knowledge', and as something which everyone will know from their own experience. Some form of training and support is essential, either during teaching practice, or as NQTs. Even then it may still be the case that some teachers will never feel comfortable with the sorts of issues which they will be asked to teach about. Such concerns are often used to support the idea that PSHE should be taught by a team of teachers who are specifically trained to do so, and who enjoy trying to deal with the more 'controversial' issues which PSHE inevitably raises.

However, many schools ask their tutors to teach PSHE to their own tutor groups. Such schools may acknowledge a lack of adequate preparation and training for new teachers, yet still take the view that above all else tutors are the most appropriate people to do so. Schools can alleviate some of the problems this may cause if they encourage tutors also to teach their subject specialism to their tutor groups. They are then able to build on relationships which are already established, making the necessary pedagogical judgements that much more effective. This is one of the main arguments against bringing in 'experts' from outside to deal with PSHE issues. Whilst their subject knowledge will most likely surpass that of a tutor, the ability of people from outside to make effective pedagogical judgements is less certain.

Pedagogical decisions required in PSHE can be more complex than those in other curriculum areas. When teachers make such judgements in the latter they can fairly accurately judge the stages that different pupils have reached, and can respond effectively to those needs. But when the subject matter is PSHE, or, for example, sex education within PSHE, such judgements can be very hard to make, even for tutors.

Differentiation in sex education can become a very delicate and highly controversial issue. All pupils have an entitlement to sex education, and many comprehensive schools offer their pupils entitlement to a far wider range of PSHE than just sex education. But entitlement to all PSHE, including sex education, is only realized if the material produced and the style of the lessons are appropriate to the particular needs of the pupils. Teachers have to make judgements about where to begin, what to teach, and then how to teach it. As always, it is the *how* upon which the what, the why and the when depend for their success.

Further, the *how* of teaching sex education lessons is an extremely difficult issue. For example, how much detail should teachers be able to go into? What sorts of videos and materials should be made available? How should discussions be organized, and how should questions be sought? Also, specifically with regard to differentiation, how are teachers to ensure that the material is appropriate and relevant to all pupils? As was seen in Chapter 4, simply to present material and information to pupils is not necessarily, indeed not very often, to realize their entitlement to it. The obligation that teachers treat pupils differently according to their particular needs, yet value those needs equally, is essential in PSHE, not only for successful lessons, but for avoiding unnecessary and painful embarrassment for pupils, some of whom will be asked to think about these issues for the first time. For example, a common technique in sex education is to ask pupils anonymously to put questions into a box, and then for the teacher to pull them out and try to deal with them. Depending on the type of question, a teacher may be required to rephrase it, or state it in a different way if all pupils are to understand the question and to get some benefit from the answer. Successful differentiation here may be seen by some parents as unnecessarily introducing children to things about which they knew nothing and, for the while, needed to know nothing.

Sex education

The 1993 Education Act removes teaching about human sexual behaviour, other than biological aspects, from the national curriculum. This includes education about HIV and AIDS. However, it also requires all secondary schools to provide sex education, including HIV and AIDS....

> Governors must ensure that any sex education given encourages pupils to 'have due regard to moral considerations and the value of family life'....
>
> They must make public details of any sex education provided, and keep this statement up to date so that parents can find out what their children are being taught about sex. A summary of the policy must be published in the school prospectus....
>
> (Abridged from the Fact Box produced by the Institute of School and College Governors, from *TES*, 1994a)

As well as professional and pedagogical problems, PSHE inevitably raises moral issues for new teachers. There is not space here to discuss the rights and wrongs, only to draw to the attention of new teachers the nature of some of the controversies.

First, in dealing with controversial subjects like sex before marriage, contraception, abortion, racism, sexism, drugs, etc., teachers have to decide the extent to which they are going to reveal their own opinions. When asked by pupils, 'What do you think?', teachers need to explain either what they think and why, or why they are not going to reveal their own opinions.

Second, should teachers, when dealing with sensitive and possibly explosive subjects, allow pupils to express their own opinions whatever the nature of those opinions? Is it possible to give equal value to all opinions? Can teachers, for example, permit the expression of rascist sympathies in their classes, or do they need to lay down clear guidelines at the beginning about the sorts of things which are and are not appropriate, and which can and cannot be said?

These sets of questions inevitably raise a third issue, that of the extent to which teachers should try and inculcate particular views into their pupils. In presenting sensitive issues, should teachers try and ensure that their own opinions play no part in judging pupils' opinions as right or wrong? Or should teachers design courses which are specifically aimed at producing a particular outcome in terms of pupils' views? Is it, even, an abrogation of responsibility for teachers to let pupils think that any opinion can be right, and that there are no overriding moral values and truths to which all must adhere?

There are no easy answers to these questions, but new teachers need to understand their importance in regard to their own practice, and to consider how they intend to try and deal with them. It can be very helpful if a school has written guidelines or policies around some of these issues. For example, the expression of rascist sympathies may be expressly forbidden in all lessons, and therefore also in PSHE. It may be, for example, that the school has decided that the best way to protect and respect the rights of all groups within the school is to curtail the right of any viewpoints which run counter to that respect.

In conclusion, it is fair to say that given the nature of PSHE, its often controversial subject matter, and its professional, pedagogical and moral complications, new teachers can find it the most challenging area of their teaching commitments. They are seldom adequately prepared or trained to deal with these challenges, yet increasingly schools are expecting them to do so in their first year(s) as teachers. The more a school values its PSHE programme, and the more carefully it has worked out its own position with regard to the teaching of sensitive issues, then the more likely are its new teachers to receive relevant guidelines and active support. At interview, new teachers, rather than acting defensively about their own insecurities and lack of experience with PSHE, might be better served asking the school how it supports its new staff in ensuring that the pupils' entitlement to PSHE is fully realized.

CHAPTER SIX

Control in the Classroom

Having comprehensive expectations

Issues of control and discipline in the classroom have been deliberately left until the final chapter of this book. They are most often the first things which new teachers worry about, yet among the last things they actually achieve.

On authority

Authority has vanished from the modern world.... The most significant symptom of the crisis, indicating its depth and seriousness, is that it has spread to such prepolitical areas as child-rearing and education, where authority in the widest sense has always been accepted as a natural necessity... Practically as well as theoretically, we are no longer in a position to know what authority really is.

(Arendt, 1968, pp.91–2)

I believe that to impose anything by authority is wrong. The child should not do anything until he comes to the opinion – his own opinion, that it should be done. The curse of humanity is the external compulsion, whether it comes from the pope or the state or the teacher or the parent. It is fascism *in toto*.

(Neill, 1961, p.11)

So far, *The New Teacher* has tried to show how comprehensive teachers have to accept a range of obligations and professional responsibilities which define their job. In particular, they have to ensure every pupil's entitlement to success in their education, and to value the educational needs of each pupil equally, whilst responding to those needs appropriately. These professional responsibilities require that teachers act as mediators when making professional decisions about how best to bring together pupil and content, and that in differentiating they do not introduce criteria which value the entitlement of one pupil as greater than that of any other. A comprehensive teacher has (in theory) an unselected intake, and must expect the widest variety of abilities, backgrounds, interests, needs and personalities. These *comprehensive expectations* are vital if teachers are to ensure that no 'types' of pupils are seen as more or less desirable, or deserving of entitlement than any other.

It has been argued above that teaching in comprehensive schools is not appropriate if pedagogical decisions give priority to curriculum content without due regard to the needs of the pupils to whom it is to be taught. Pedagogical judgements therefore have their own internal 'discipline' with regard to what is sensible and appropriate. Particular types of material or teaching approaches may be wholly inappropriate for particular pupils, and each 'disciplines' or limits teachers with regard to what is and is not sensible or relevant. The knowledge which teachers have of their pupils and of their curriculum areas defines the boundaries within which teachers know they can work sensibly and effectively. It is within the discipline imposed on teachers by pupils and curriculum that pedagogical judgements, including differentiation, are made.

Exactly the same is true for decisions made regarding discipline or *control in the classroom*. Gaining control in the classroom, successfully and effectively, is a pedagogical issue and not simply a matter of domination and punishment. Control is the culmination of a number of other factors which teachers have to get right. Control is lost if the pedagogical balance between pupil and content is too heavily weighted in favour of one at the expense of the other. Control is threatened if some pupils' abilities are seen to be valued by teachers as of greater worth than others. Control is at best illusory and at worst impossible, if the expectations placed on pupils are unrelated to, and therefore inappropriate to who they are and what they can and cannot do. Just as comprehensive teachers are required to have comprehensive expectations of their pupils' academic abilities, so they are also required to have comprehensive expectations of their levels of cooperation and motivation and the variety of their personalities. The implications of comprehensive expectations for planning, for relationships, for pedagogy, for differentiation and for tutoring have been explored in the preceding chapters. Their implications for control in the classroom are the substance of this final chapter.

What is control?

Control in the history of schooling has been largely associated with discipline and punishment. Evidence that control and punishment have always enjoyed the most intimate of relationships in the classroom is abundant. In ancient Greece and in the Roman Empire the flogging of school pupils was daily routine, and common for pupils who made mistakes with grammar, with the memorization of long poems, or who just displayed boredom with their lessons. Punishment as routine was institutionalized in the monasteries of the Middle Ages. It aimed at securing a relationship with God appropriate to the relative stations of the Almighty and of the most unworthy individuals. The greater the suffering of the latter, the truer was their relationship to the former. This tradition of punishment passed into the schools of the Middle Ages and the Renaissance, and has defined 'control' in schools ever since. For as long as education required its pupils to submit themselves to learning by heart the grammatical laws of ancient tongues and to repeating large passages from the Scriptures, those pupils were subjected also to a staggering range and variety of brutal and barbaric methods of control to ensure that they did so (see pp.46-7). In many of these cases, hand in hand with causing pain was the idea that it was, in the long run, in the best interests of the pupils, and that they should be grateful for it, or, better still, actually seek punishment for their own inevitable failings.

On discipline

The discipline of most of our schools has always been a thing of which I have disapproved. If they had erred on the side of indulgence, they might have erred less lamentably. But they are inevitable gaols in which imprisoned youth loses all discipline by being punished before it has done anything wrong. Visit one of these colleges when the lessons are in progress; you hear nothing but the cries of children being beaten and of masters drunk with anger. What a way of arousing an appetite for learning in these young and timid minds, to lead them to it with a terrifying visage and an armful of rods. This is a pernicious system.

(Montaigne, 1958, p.73, written 1580)

England, too, had its champion floggers. Perhaps most memorable was Dr. Keate, headmaster of Eton from 1809–1834, around whom many legends have grown. It was said that in his 60th year he still found energy to flog 80 boys in one day.

(Evans, 1975, p.48)

There was leathering pupils for making mistakes in spelling.... I accepted the rule that the teacher had to be the master all the time, and I can remember my perpetual fear that one day the class would get beyond my control.

(Neill, 1939, pp.11–12)

> Too often, it is true, people conceive of school discipline so as to preclude endowing it with such an important moral function. Some see in it a simple way of guaranteeing superficial peace and order in the classroom... In reality, however, the nature and function of school discipline is something altogether different.... It is the morality of the classroom, just as the discipline of the social body is morality, properly speaking.
>
> (Durkheim, 1973, p.148)
>
> Moral authority is the dominant quality of the educator.... It is not necessary to show that authority, thus understood, is neither violent nor repressive; it consists entirely of a certain moral ascendency.
>
> (Durkheim, 1956, p.88)

These failings, however, were and are defined by what the pupils were being asked to do. If, today, the National Curriculum demanded of all pupils at KS2 that they be able to repeat Homer's *Iliad* word for word in front of their teacher and fellow pupils, then many pupils would undoubtedly fail. And if it were still the case that the flogging of pupils was permitted by law, which it is not, then many, many pupils would suffer such a punishment. The point is that it is the curriculum, with its prescriptions about what *has* to be done, which, at the same time, defines what is to constitute success and failure. And if failure merits punishment, then it is the curriculum which determines the criteria upon which punishment is to be meted out. In such a classroom, control would be achieved when all pupils were doing what the curriculum prescribed that they should do. Control would be lost when these prescriptions were transgressed and would be regained when, once again, the class, through fear of another punishment, returned to obeying the discipline of their curriculum.

Such an example, and such reasoning, is no longer appropriate or relevant to the obligation of the comprehensive teacher to provide equal value and entitlement to educational success for each pupil. Therefore, new teachers entering the profession are required to reflect carefully on what control in the classroom actually means. It is no longer professional to presume that the responsibility for 'failure' lies with the pupil and not with the content of the lesson, the design of the course, or the pedagogical methods employed by the teacher. Nor is it, therefore, professional to punish a pupil for failure. Failure is defined by what pupils are asked to do. It is now the professional responsibility of the teacher to ensure that they ask pupils to learn in ways in which they *can* succeed, and to engineer success in education and not failure. As seen in Chapter 4, differentiation is a key strategy in bringing this about. Gone are the days when control in the classroom means forcing pupils to submit to undifferentiated curriculum content and then punishing them, when really it was the work which was inappropriate and irrelevant.

With the renewed interest in child-centred and experiential learning, the needs of the pupil have played a much greater and more significant part in defining educational practice. However, pedagogical judgements in comprehensive schools now have to be made by balancing those needs against the prescriptions of the National Curriculum. Even though this curriculum is set down in law, nevertheless the teacher's responsibility is still to ensure that the curriculum does not exert an exclusive right of control over pupils, but that the curriculum is itself 'controlled' or managed by teachers so that it respects the comprehensive needs and abilities of their particular pupils. Despite the National Curriculum, or perhaps because of it, it is no longer exclusively the child which needs to be controlled for and on behalf of the curriculum, but rather the curriculum which also needs to be controlled for and on behalf of each pupil.

To sum up, then, classroom control is implicitly contained in the pedagogical and professional judgements which teachers have to make in bringing pupil and content together. Control and discipline are no longer linked only to failure and punishment; control in the classroom is now a matter of encouragement, enablement, reward and praise; and in terms of classroom practice, it is a matter of differentiation, of relevant and appropriate teaching methods, of equal value relationships and of getting the balance between the needs of pupil and curriculum right so that the requirements of *both* are met. In this sense control has become less a matter of external discipline and force for the teacher, and more a case for pedagogical *self*-discipline by the teacher. Teachers have to learn to accept that the limitations of their pupils and the potential development of their pupils determines and defines what teachers can sensibly ask them to do. Teachers are themselves *controlled* in the classroom by the boundaries which pupils and the curriculum place upon them. To exert control in comprehensive education, teachers must therefore discipline themselves to understand and accept the limits of being 'in the middle' between pupil and curriculum.

What is bad behaviour?

> [Students] were not dangerously aggressive, but either excessively uninhibited or bored. Some (says Plutarch) interrupted with commendatory exclamations at anything of which they approved, whilst others wore a supercilious expression as though they could have done better themselves.

85

Some listened impassively, some nodded as if they understood to conceal their lack of comprehension, others raised objections, or plied the lecturer with unnecessary and irrelevant questions, some grinned when the subject was serious, some frowned, some had a roving eye, some twisted uncomfortably in their seats, some whispered, and some yawned sleepily.

(Bonner, 1977, p.142)

In the reorganisation of elementary teaching... the increase in the number of their pupils, the absence of methods for regulating simultaneously the activity of the whole class, and the disorder and confusion that followed from this made it necessary to work out a system of supervision.... A relation of surveillance, defined and regulated, is inscribed at the heart of the practice of teaching, not as an additional or adjacent part, but as a mechanism that is inherent to it and which increases its efficiency.

(Foucault, 1977, pp.175–6)

When new teachers think about classroom control they reflect mostly on problems which they expect to have with the behaviour of pupils. But behaviour in classrooms is not something which can be divorced from other aspects of teaching, and new teachers, and student teachers in particular, need to understand that all aspects of classroom practice are related. *Behaviour,* good or bad, is often the *result* of pedagogical decisions made by teachers. Levels of planning and preparation, quality of resources and activities, quality of relationships, appropriate teaching styles, adequate differentiation, and definitions of success and failure can all contribute to, and even cause, good or bad behaviour. If teachers are exercising appropriate control in bringing pupil and curriculum together, then part of what is implicitly 'controlled' is the likely response by pupils to what they are being asked to do. Often, 'bad' pupil behaviour is the result of a lack of control by the teacher over the appropriateness of pupil and lesson for each other.

Good and bad behaviour are also the result of teacher expectations, and of school definitions. They are *relative* concepts. Acceptable behaviour in one classroom may not be so in another, and things may be allowed, even encouraged in one school but outlawed in another. Pupils can be labelled as deviant, troublesome, uncooperative and non-conformist if, in a school with strict uniform codes, they deliberately wear jewellery or make-up; whereas in a school without such restrictions pupils can do exactly the same thing but not be labelled in any negative way. The same is true of schools' expectations of behaviour. What is unacceptable and punished in one school may not receive the same treatment, or be defined in the same way as in another school. Therefore a pupil can be labelled as behaving well or badly, not solely because of what they are doing, but more because of the institution in which they are doing it.

Closely related to the idea that good and bad behaviour are relative labels, dependent upon the school in which they occur, is the recognition that definitions of good and bad behaviour also differ in different sorts of lessons and classrooms within the same school. What is appropriate in a workshop with potentially dangerous tools and machinery is absolutely not what is appropriate in a drama room. In a P.E. lesson pupils who remain seated and do not run around may be seen to be behaving badly whereas, in a history lesson, exactly the opposite is the case.

Equally, not all teachers in the same kinds of lessons expect the same kinds of behaviour from their pupils. It is becoming common now for schools to develop policies which state in broad terms the expectations they have of all their pupils at all times, but it is still not the case that pupils will experience absolute consistency in all of their lessons. Indeed, given that lessons should be designed around pupil and content, a set formula of expectations for behaviour in all lessons may not be appropriate. In making pedagogical decisions, teachers have to ensure that their expectations with regard to behaviour are relevant and appropriate to the type of lesson they have planned, rather than plan all their lessons to fit in with a pre-written set of rigid expectations.

Teachers, in planning their lessons, are at the same time also defining what will count in those lessons as good and bad behaviour. By deciding what pupils will do in lessons, they are also defining what they expect of pupils in those lessons. Lesson plans, including pedagogical decisions about how the lessons are to be taught, define for the pupils appropriate and inappropriate behaviour. Put simply, appropriate behaviour is that which meets the expectations which the lesson plan has of the pupils.

In this sense, new teachers can begin to understand the issue of good and bad behaviour in a pedagogical, professional and therefore *comprehensive* way. Just as pedagogical decisions have to balance the needs of curriculum and pupil with regard to what pupils can and cannot be expected to achieve, so the same is true of decisions regarding what is and is not acceptable behaviour in a classroom. Teachers have to construct their lessons keeping in mind not only the 'academic' and 'pastoral' needs of their pupils, but equally the needs that anyone would have faced with similar situations. Expectations of behaviour have to be realistic if they are to be effective. Most people, not only children, do not like to sit for hours listening to someone else. They fidget, they whisper to their neighbours, they doodle, and they seek distractions – the very behaviour which is so often punished in pupils.

In addition, some element of differentiation is essential if teachers are to work according to their comprehensive expectations of pupils, rather than working according to a fantasy image of 'the perfect classroom'. If all lessons are compared to the latter, then most if not all lessons will be unsatisfactory. It is the case that good lessons are defined in relation to the pupils that are actually in them, not in relation to the 'ideal' pupils. Therefore, in constructing lessons, and in defining expectations of appropriate and inappropriate behaviour, teachers have to take into account the realities of the pupils they are to teach. Unrealistic expectations of their behaviour are unhelpful because they automatically define and create certain pupils as deviants and troublemakers, etc. Expectations of behaviour and the realities of groups and individuals have to be weighed against each other by teachers when they plan lessons and when they define appropriate and inappropriate behaviour within those lessons.

It follows, then, that the expectations in some lessons will differ from those in others, depending on the group, the individuals and the type of work which has to be done. Again, pedagogical judgements here require decisions by teachers regarding the pupils and the larger environment. In a workshop, safety takes precedence over pupils and requires strict and invariable expectations of behaviour. In a geography lesson expectations can vary according to the type of lesson and according to the different sorts of tasks which are set. In a drama lesson, pupil freedom of movement and expression may take precedence over more 'usual' expectations of behaviour. In short, in making pedagogical judgements about good and bad behaviour in any one lesson, some differentiation is required in order to take account of the expectations of particular subjects and particular environments and balance those against the needs, interests and successful working practices of each group, and of individual pupils.

Go in hard and shout a lot

So far, the discussion of control in the classroom has been somewhat abstract for student teachers who, about to enter a classroom for the first time, fear that perhaps nobody will actually listen to anything they say, or do anything they ask them to. They are understandably more interested to know how to get control of pupils who are determined to be uncooperative. However, what the discussion has tried to set out for student teachers is that control is part of the whole activity of teaching and cannot be isolated from other aspects of practice. Student teachers always need to see control in the classroom as related to planning, to relationships, to pedagogy, to differentiation and to comprehensive expectations. If all those are in place, then classroom management becomes a great deal easier and more effective and relevant.

Student teachers are often told that, in the first instance, they need to 'go in hard'. For many new teachers this is inevitably interpreted to mean 'shout a lot'. There are a number of reasons why such advice, and such an approach, can undermine the attempts of the new teacher to establish any kind of satisfactory working (or professional) relationships.

First, to 'go in hard' represents the view that control in the classroom is something achieved over pupils without regard to the appropriate and relevant nature of the lesson content. It suggests to the new teacher that control over pupils can be achieved through fear and power rather than through interest, enthusiasm and motivation for carefully prepared lessons. It is a one-way view of control, where the pupil is subject to the discipline of the teacher, but the teacher is not subject to the pedagogical discipline of the pupils or of the lesson content.

Second, the ability to 'go in hard' is not high on every new teacher's list of personal skills or qualities. If it was all that successful teaching depended upon, then many good teachers who do not teach in this way would never have lasted in the profession. In addition, it is an approach which has a high cost in terms of personal energy, and the tensions and stress which accompany it can soon exhaust the practitioner.

Third, there are many teachers who would simply take the view that teaching through bullying is the least effective and least acceptable method which can be adopted. It reproduces a blatant inconsistency that teachers are able to tell pupils that bullying is wrong whilst practising just such behaviour themselves. In terms of motivation, it encourages pupils to work for negative reasons, that is, for fear of being chastised rather than for positive reasons based on their own interest and enthusiasm.

Non-rejection of the pupil

The teacher must be totally realistic in identifying the problem and must control his emotional response to the fact in such a way that he does not reject the child.

The attitude of forgiving which I am trying to describe will express itself in quite practical ways. For example, action to correct the child will not be foregone, but the teacher will avoid actions, such as public humiliation before other children, likely to destroy the relationship between the child and himself.

Although he may tell the child he has lied he will not call him a liar, since this implies an invincible trait for which there is no hope of remedy.

(Daunt, 1975, pp.89, 90)

In addition to these worries, 'going in hard' can make the chances of success in the classroom that much harder for the new teacher to achieve. Chapter 2 discussed the different methods of forming relationships with new classes, and this approach of going in hard to begin with is antithetical to an approach which seeks to develop relationships slowly. Having to tell pupils off *is* part of the job of the teacher, but it is a skill that has to be learnt along with other skills. It is not simply a question of shouting at pupils. Shouting, if and when it is required, is most effective when used very rarely, and should always be exercised with self-control. To tell new teachers to use this strategy straight away, and as often as they like, is to rob them of a strategy which they may need at other times and on more important occasions. If new teachers reduce the effectiveness of shouting by its continued use in situations in which it is not appropriate or needed, then it is *not* available to them when they do need it and when it *is* appropriate. Knowing when shouting is and is not appropriate, (and it is not very often) is something which all teachers come to learn from experience.

In place of the advice 'go in hard and shout a lot', new teachers are better served by a more professional and comprehensive approach to achieving control in the classroom. At a general level, as has been pointed out at the beginning of this chapter, a professional understanding of control does not separate it off from the needs and demands of the pupils or of the curriculum. Control is not achieved in spite of these considerations: it is achieved through them and because of them. New teachers introduced to the issue of control in this way will not, therefore, be encouraged to 'go in hard' but rather to prepare thoroughly, to get to know the needs and abilities of their pupils, and to plan for differentiation. It is with these pedagogical skills that control is achieved and maintained in a way likely to encourage the success of all pupils.

Establishing a presence

> ### The tin god
> I refuse to be classified as a teacher. Think what a tin god a teacher really is. He is the centre of the picture; he commands and he is obeyed; he metes out justice.
>
> (Neill, in Lamb, 1992, p.101)

However, on the most practical level, there are certain basic skills and control techniques which new teachers, and in particular student teachers, are expected to be able to perform in order to achieve and maintain good classroom control. Above all, student teachers have to show mentors and pupils that they are capable of establishing their presence within a group of people, in ways which elicit the support rather than the resentment of the group. There are some everyday routines and practices which mentors look for their student teachers to learn, to accept, and then to perform as second nature.

With regard to achieving control, the first point to make is that student teachers may not have to. If they are taking over a lesson half-way through, or even from the beginning, it may be the case that a controlled situation already exists. What student teachers are required to do in this case is *maintain* that control, and not do anything which will undermine it. In most cases, however, and for a wide variety of reasons, some level of control will have to be achieved.

Student teachers need to be prepared for their lessons. This means not only having devised and planned an appropriate lesson, but having prepared everything which is required for the lesson. The teacher needs to be in control of the lesson from the start by ensuring that everything that is needed is available. This includes the layout of the room (where appropriate), materials, tools, handouts, instruments, paper/books, whatever. (Very) limited resources, however, are a fact of life in many schools, and if there are insufficient numbers of what is required then the sharing arrangements need to be made very clear from the beginning. If the teacher is relying on pupils to bring things to the lesson, things without which the pupil will not be able to participate, then it is good planning to have a few spares tucked away on the assumption that someone is *bound* to forget. This may seem like 'letting them off' for failing to do what they were asked to do, but consider this in relation to three further points. First, whilst teacher and pupil are arguing about the issue, class time for everyone else is being wasted. Second, a pupil prevented from taking part in the lesson still has to do *something*. Third, if the lesson is important and all pupils are entitled to it, then having spares ready in advance is a way of ensuring that entitlement for all.

It helps student teachers achieve control if they can arrive at their lessons before the pupils – although this is not always possible. There is a tendency for whoever arrives first to be able to impose their will on the situation, and if that is the pupils, then teachers inevitably have to work harder in imposing theirs so that lessons can begin.

Perhaps the most common mistake made by inexperienced teachers is to announce that they are not going to begin until the pupils are quiet, and then to begin without having achieved it. Mentors will expect new teachers who ask for quiet to show that they mean it and intend to get it. All sorts of messages, unhelpful to the teacher, are picked up by pupils who see teachers saying things, insisting on things, even threatening things, which they do not mean. A student teacher who asks for quiet must wait until everyone is quiet before he or she begins. It is one of the most fundamental and basic ways in which teachers can show that they have established their presence in the classroom. Occasionally this may mean teachers having to wait for what seems like an embarrassingly long time. But patience is often rewarded and can be backed up by a firm reminder and a look which says, 'I have waited long enough.' If, having begun to talk, the teacher is interrupted, then it is good practice to break off and wait, in order to show a willingness to continue *only* when the conditions are acceptable.

Once quiet is achieved it must be used to good purpose and not wasted. It is good practice, at the start of a lesson, to give a very quick summary of the lesson as a whole, and perhaps a reminder of how it fits into the course overall or is related to the previous lesson. Attention spans are notoriously brief, so the experienced teacher will give very clear, very precise and very concise instructions. If pupils are confused about what is required of them, it may not be because they did not listen; it may in fact be because the instructions they were given were not thought out and expressed clearly enough.

Questions from pupils can often seem very threatening to new teachers who, having planned carefully what they are going to say, can be easily thrown off track by 'interruptions'. It is in the interests of teachers (and their pupils) to explain clearly *when* questions can be asked, and then to ensure that this is kept to. It may be that teachers do not wish for questions during explanations, only at the end. Most importantly, pupils who call out questions against the wishes of the teacher should not have their questions dealt with, and need to be reminded when the appropriate time for such questions will be.

New teachers often create their own problems in classrooms in the ways that they ask questions of their pupils. In particular, when teachers ask a question which invites answers from the whole class, a very common reaction is for some hands to go up, and for various pupils to shout out their answers. It is for the teacher, again, to explain clearly what is required from pupils in answering questions – for example, putting hands up and not shouting out – and, as always, to stick to it. To demand that no pupils are to call out, and then to take an answer which is called out, is to give the message to pupils that the teacher does not mean what he or she says. However, asking questions of a whole class is a difficult skill for most teachers as it requires a great deal of cooperation from pupils. New teachers, particularly early on in their practice, may prefer to direct questions at particular pupils, or even avoid questioning a whole class altogether, preferring to work in smaller, more manageable groups.

New teachers can also cause problems in their classrooms by demanding from their pupils things which the latter have not been led to expect in the lesson. It is helpful to try and avoid surprises. Student teachers should, at the start of their lessons, be able to prepare their pupils for all the different stages of the lesson, all the different ways of working and types of work that will be required, and the various ways they will be expected to behave depending upon the activities they are engaged in. This includes announcing at the start the arrangements for packing away at the end. Pupils do not always react well to things if it looks as if their teachers are making things up as they go along, and pupils are better prepared for different types of working if given advance notice. It is often necessary to interrupt a group in the middle of their work, but this should not be regarded lightly. Such interruptions will not be welcomed by pupils if they feel that their work has been stopped for no good reason.

Finally, new teachers are well advised to steer clear of the jokey or lighthearted approach, until, or unless, good relationships have been firmly established.

Such strategies become second nature for experienced teachers. They are exactly the sorts of skills and techniques which mentors look for in the classroom practice of new teachers. They reveal new teachers to be developing their understanding of classroom management and in particular they show to mentors and pupils that the teacher is prepared to accept the responsibility of establishing his or her presence in order to ensure entitlement to learning.

Classroom management

Our survey shows that teachers see talking out of turn and other forms of persistent, low-level disruption as the most frequent and wearing kinds of classroom misbehaviour.

There is... a broad measure of agreement on what a teacher needs to be fully effective. Knowledge of the subject to be taught is obviously crucial. So is the ability to plan and deliver a lesson which flows smoothly and holds pupils' attention. The third area of competence comprises a range of skills associated with managing groups of pupils. It includes the ability to relate to young people, to encourage them in good behaviour and learning, and to deal calmly but firmly with inappropriate or disruptive behaviour.

Teachers with good group management skills are able to establish positive relationships with their classes based on mutual respect.... They can also spot a disruptive incident in the making, choose an appropriate tactic to deal with it and nip it in the bud. They always seem to know what is going on behind their backs.

Our evidence suggests... that there are teachers who lack confidence in their own ability to deal with disruption and who see their classes as potentially hostile. They create a negative classroom atmosphere by frequent criticism and rare praise. They make use of loud public reprimands and threats. They are sometimes sarcastic. They tend to react aggressively to minor incidents. Their methods increase the danger of a major confrontation not only with individual pupils but with the whole class.

...teachers' group management skills are probably the single most important factor in achieving good standards of classroom behaviour... [and] those skills can be taught and learned.

[In applying the principles of good classroom management teachers should] make sparing and consistent use of reprimands. This means being firm rather than aggressive, targetting the right pupil, criticising the behaviour and not the person, using private rather than public reprimands whenever possible, being fair and consistent, and avoiding sarcasm and idle threats.

[Only] make sparing and consistent use of punishment. This includes avoiding whole group punishments which pupils see as unfair. It also means avoiding punishments which humiliate pupils by, for example, making them look ridiculous.

(abridged from The Elton Report, 1989)

There are also things mentors hope *not* to see from new teachers with regard to classroom control. Most obvious is a classroom characterized by constant shouting from the teacher. The need to shout most often indicates weaknesses in other areas of practice, perhaps with planning and preparation, with establishing relationships, or with the choice of teaching method or material. Shouting also tends to suggest a lack of awareness with regard to other 'control' techniques. Some misdemeanours or interruptions are best dealt with by moments of silence from the teacher, an unamused expression, a look, before moving on. In this case the culprit is not acknowledged verbally at all. This can be an unexpectedly successful method of dealing with minor interruptions. It has the advantage of playing down situations. Student teachers who, through inept handling of minor incidents, manage to turn them into full-blown confrontations are not proving that they can manage situations very effectively. Student teachers who consistently make situations worse than they are or need to be, will be causing their mentors to question whether their skills in the classroom are of an appropriate level.

Sometimes a stare, or stating a pupil's name, is enough to 'deal' with something. It is often the case that all pupils require to know is that they have been noticed and acknowledged. There is little need and little to be gained from breaking into a long tirade to pupils about their behaviour. It disturbs teachers from doing what they ought to be doing and is, in most cases, a supremely ineffective method of establishing or maintaining good working relationships between teachers and pupils.

These sorts of techniques, along with favourite qualities like a sense of humour, caring attitude, etc., do not figure in lists of competences. Nevertheless mentors do look for student teachers to adopt them instinctively into their practice. The 'stare', the 'look', the raised eyebrow, the one word, the 'wait', and the 'name' – all are control techniques which, unlike shouting, will usually not make situations worse and, more positively, will help to ensure a steady, unbroken rhythm and pace to the lesson.

Conclusion

Who or what is the new teacher? First, the new teacher is anyone who is new to the profession, either as a student teacher or as an NQT. Second, the new teacher is the comprehensive teacher. This teacher has to face the challenges of universal entitlement in non-selective schools and no one should be surprised that these challenges have yet to be fully understood or overcome. The grammar schools and the independent schools, after some 600 years of practice, reached a point where their product and their clientele were very closely matched. But the product was marketed at a very small minority of children. The new teacher, in the new system, has to develop practices and policies which serve the educational needs of *all* children.

Third, therefore, the new teacher is the comprehensive teacher if and when they are prepared to be a teacher *and* a learner. The most important quality required of new teachers is to *respond* to the needs of the pupils they find in front of them. New teachers are not 'lords and masters' of the classroom; they are not free to teach whatever they wish, however they wish, to whomsoever they wish. Although *what* they teach is now largely prescribed by the National Curriculum, nevertheless new teachers' pedagogical decisions are formed in and by their recognition of the abilities, talents, interests and needs of their pupils. This means learning about those pupils and from them, in order to make their decisions appropriate and relevant.

The decision to become a teacher is no longer what it once was. Teaching is no longer a profession which dons gowns, makes pupils stand up when 'masters' enter the room, or lectures in silent classrooms to rows of passive pupils. It is no longer a profession which can pretend that pupils do not have minds and personalities of their own, and do not have rights, entitlements and needs. It is no longer a profession which merely controls; it is now one which serves its pupils and their parents.

'Serve', here, is a dangerous word. For supporters of the principle of the free market in education, it looks ideal – teachers serving their customers. But teachers serve the community precisely because they do *not* charge. The service is given free, to all, according to need, and in the best interests, as far as is possible, of individuals and communities. The work of the teacher is always for another. This is its ethical dimension.

It is because the job is no longer simply about mastery in the classroom, but also service, that the tasks required of teachers have grown so enormously – without the necessary training being given for these new roles. The new teacher thinks not only about control, discipline, order and punishment; not only about subject knowledge, grammar, punctuation, examination results, levels of attainment and league tables. Now, also, their pupils require them to think about entitlement (in theory and in practice), differentiation, teaching methods/styles/approaches; and about personal and social education, welfare, bullying, tutoring, employment, further and higher education, equal opportunities, discrimination, prejudice, poverty, parental influence and support... etc.

It is not a list that should deter the new teacher. Far from it. It is a list which finally gives an answer to the dreaded question asked of those who would join the profession, 'Why do you want to teach?' The somewhat weak response, 'Because I like working with children' can have a far more substantial political and ethical content than that. Teach in order to make a difference, teach in order to serve the community, teach in order to assist the development of others, teach in order to value people, and above all, teach in order to learn.

References

Arendt, H. (1968) *Between Past and Future,* Harmondsworth: Penguin.

Augustine (1907) *Confessions,* London: Dent.

Beck, F.A.G. (1964) *Greek Education,* London: Methuen.

Binder, F.M. (1970) *Education in the History of Western Civilisation,* New York: Collier Macmillan.

Blishen, E. (1969) *The School that I'd Like,* Harmondsworth, Penguin.

Bonner, S.F. (1977) *Education in Ancient Rome,* London: Methuen.

Comenius, J.A. (1910) *The Great Didactic,* London: A. & C. Black.

Cox, C.B. and Dyson, A.E. (1971) *The Black Papers on Education,* London: Davis and Poynter.

Cox, C.B. and Dyson, A.E. (1977) *Black Papers 1977,* London: Temple Smith.

Cubberley, E.P. (1920) *The History of Education,* Cambridge (Mass): Houghton Mifflin.

Daunt, P. (1975) *Comprehensive Values,* London: Heinemann.

DES (1967) *Children and Their Primary Schools* (The Plowden Report), London: HMSO.

DfE (1992) *Initial Teacher Training (Second Phase),* Circular No. 9/92, London: DfE.

Dewey, J. (1963) *Experience and Education,* New York: Collier.

Dickens, C. (1969) *Hard Times,* Harmondsworth: Penguin.

Durkheim, E. (1956) *Education and Sociology,* New York: The Free Press.

Durkheim, E. (1973) *Moral Education,* New York: The Free Press.

Elton (1989) *Discipline in Schools* (The Elton Report), London: HMSO.

Entwistle, H. (1988) *Styles of Teaching and Learning,* London: David Fulton.

Evans, K. (1975) *The Development and Structure of the English Educational System,* London: University of London Press.

Foucault, M. (1977) *Discipline and Punish,* Harmondsworth: Penguin.

Freire, P. (1972) *Pedagogy of the Oppressed,* Harmondsworth: Penguin.

Hargreaves, D.H. (1975) *Interpersonal Relations and Education,* London: RKP.

Hargreaves, A. and Woods, P. (1984) *Classrooms and Staffrooms,* Buckingham: Open University Press.

Hegel, G.W.F. (1977) *Phenomenology of Spirit,* Oxford: Oxford University Press.

Hegel, G.W.F. (1984) *The Letters* (trans. C. Butler and C. Seiler), Indiana: Bloomington Press.

HMI (1989) *Personal and Social Education from 5 to 16,* Curriculum Matters 14, London: HMSO.

Krell, D.F. (1977) *Martin Heidegger: Basic Writings,* London: RKP.

Lamb, A. (1992) *The New Summerhill,* Harmondsworth: Penguin.

Lawson, J. and Silver, H. (1973) *A Social History of Education in England,* London: Methuen.

Leach, A.F. (1911) *Educational Charters 598 – 1909,* Cambridge: Cambridge University Press.

Mackenzie, M. (1909) *Hegel's Educational Theory and Practice,* London: Swann Sonnenschein.

Mahaffey, J.P. (1881) *Old Greek Education,* London: Kegan Paul Trench and Co.

Major, J. (1993) Doc. 251/93, London: Conservative Research Department.

Marland, M. (1974) *Pastoral Care,* London: Heinemann.

Marland, M. (1989) *The Tutor and the Tutor Group,* Harlow: Longman.

Monroe, P. (1905) *A Text-Book in the History of Education,* New York: MacMillan.

Montaigne, M. (1958) *Essays,* Harmondsworth: Penguin.

Montessori, M. (1920) *The Montessori Method,* Oxford: Heinemann.

Neill, A.S. (1939) *The Problem Teacher,* London: Herbert Jenkins.

Neill, A.S. (1961) *Summerhill,* Harmondsworth: Penguin.

Nietzsche, F. (1982) *Daybreak,* Cambridge: Cambridge University Press.

Orme, N. (1973) *English Schools in the Middle Ages,* London: Methuen.

Otty, N. (1972) *Learner Teacher,* Harmondsworth: Penguin.

Parry, A.W. (1920) *Education in England in the Middle Ages,* London: University Tutorial Press.

Pedley, R. (1969) *The Comprehensive School,* Harmondsworth: Penguin.

Plato (1956) *Protagoras,* Harmondsworth: Penguin.

Plato (1987) *Theaetetus,* Harmondsworth: Penguin.

Plato (1992) *The Republic,* London: Dent.

Plutarch (1914) *Lives, Volume 1,* Oxford: Heinemann.

Richmond, K. W. (1978) *Education in Britain since 1944,* London: Methuen.

Rogers, C. (1969) *Freedom to Learn,* Ohio: Merrill.

Rousseau, J.J. (1974) *Emile,* London: Dent.

Silver, P. and Silver, H. (1974) *The Education of the Poor,* London: RKP.

Simon, B. (1974) *The Politics of Educational Reform, 1920 – 1940,* London: Lawrence and Wishart.

Simon, B. (1991) *Education and the Social Order,* London: Lawrence and Wishart.

Smail, W.M. (1938) *Quintilian on Education,* Oxford: Clarendon Press.

Smith, A. (1977) *Wealth of Nations,* London: Dent.

Sylvester, D.W. (1974) *Robert Lowe and Education,* Cambridge: Cambridge University Press.

TES (1994a) New rules on sex education, 14 October, Governors Guide, p.x.

TES (1994b) Team spirit looks set to win match, 4 November, p.3.

TES (1994c) Team talk for key players, 2 December, p.8.

TES (1994d) Shape up without a slog on the pitch, 18 November, p.9.

TES (1994e) Child abuse procedures, 14 October, Governors Guide, p.x.

Watts, J. (1974) *Teaching,* Newton Abbot: David and Charles.

Wollstonecraft, M. (1992) *A Vindication of the Rights of Women,* Harmondsworth: Penguin.

Index